WALKING GOD'S PATH

WALKING GOD'S PATH

the Life & Ministry of

JIMMY DRAPER

by JOHN PERRY

BROADMAN
& HOLMAN
PUBLISHERS

NASHVILLE, TENNESSEE

Ten-Digit ISBN: 0–8054–2549–7
Thirteen-Digit ISBN: 978–08054–2549–9

Published by Broadman & Holman Publishers
Nashville, Tennessee

Dewey Decimal Classification: B
Subject Heading: DRAPER, JAMES T., JR. \
CLERGY–BIOGRAPHY

Scripture quotations are taken from the Holman Christian
Standard Bible® Copyright © 1999, 2000, 2002, 2004 by
Holman Bible Publishers. Used by permission.

1 2 3 4 5 6 7 8 9 10 10 09 08 07 06 05

CONTENTS

PREFACE

T HERE IS A Jimmy Draper who has been introduced at countless revivals, retreats, conventions, seminars, lectures, broadcasts, banquets, and celebrations. He's a beloved pastor, former
seminary trustee, former president of the 16-plus-million-member
Southern Baptist Convention, and current president of LifeWay
Christian Resources, the $400-plus-million publishing and com-
munications arm of the SBC.

That is the Jimmy Draper thousands have met and millions
have looked to for leadership over the past fifty years. *Walking
God's Path* will, I hope, introduce another Jimmy Draper: the one
who dedicated his life to Christian service before he entered high
school; held his first pastorate at twenty; baptized a felon on his
deathbed and African converts in the Indian Ocean; and stood
steadfast for biblical integrity against long odds at pivotal
moments in denominational history. Also the one who defended
himself from a toilet paper invasion by masterminding a rooftop
garden hose counterattack; whose 1970s-era orange running
shorts were the talk of the family; and whose self-deprecating
good humor is legendary among his close friends.

Jimmy grew up during the idyllic 1940s and 1950s when
America was for the most part peaceful and prosperous. The

world has changed immeasurably since then. The racial unrest of the 1960s, the war protests that followed, the era of "free love" and the public abandonment of traditional Christian morality have transformed the culture. Yet Jimmy Draper is the same man he was twenty years or fifty years ago. Consistency is a hallmark of his life. And it's a characteristic that makes perfect sense when one stops to reflect that from his earliest days Christ has been the center of his personality, his reason for doing everything he has done.

Jimmy has remained constant because Christianity is constant. Its truths and admonitions are the same today as they were in the 1950s—or in the 1650s for that matter, when the Draper ancestors were just settling in America from the British Isles. Christianity's eternal promises are constant as well, which should inspire us all to walk God's path so faithfully.

Soli deo gloria.

John Perry
Nashville, Tennessee

CHAPTER 1

HOT IN HOUSTON

TENSION HAD BEEN BUILDING on the floor of the cavernous convention center since the opening gavel. More than ten thousand messengers now swarmed around the space, forming tight huddles that held momentarily, then dissolved as the participants scattered, looking hurriedly for other people and other groups. Some of the impromptu meetings lasted only moments; others developed into full-fledged strategy sessions.

There was important business ahead, and for most of the men and women gathered in Houston on that hot June day in 1979, the business boiled down to making sure a certain man was elected president, or making sure he wasn't.

Behind the scenes there were accusations of improper credentials, coercion, influence peddling, strong arming, and slander; charges and countercharges against small-minded special interests, inflexible legalism, and destructive juggernauts.

Yes, this year's annual meeting of the Southern Baptist Convention promised to be quite a show.

Summers were always hot in Houston, and one of the hottest places in town that week was surely the Summit, home of the

Houston Rockets basketball team in season, a giant square, glass-walled arena looming over an isolated sea of concrete off the Southwest Freeway. True, the air inside was comfortably cool, but the political atmosphere was hotter than the Texas jalapeño peppers stacked on the snack vendors' pushcarts. Southern Baptists, polarized as they had seldom been in their 134-year history, had convened to elect a new president.

As far as Jimmy Draper was concerned, they could leave all the politics behind. He'd had enough of that in the last few years to last a lifetime. But behind the politics in this case lurked challenges to a bedrock belief of the Christian faith that Jimmy and his like-minded colleagues could not allow to go unanswered. It was something he could easily avoid if he wanted to. His own ministry at First Baptist Church, Euless, Texas, was all a pastor could hope for both personally and professionally. There he felt a spirit of concord and mutual respect that sometimes made the larger denominational crisis seem far away. Yet here he was, prepared to dive into the swirling sea of denominational factionalism on the convention floor because he was convinced that his life-long beliefs as a Christian and a Southern Baptist were under attack, and that electing the right kind of leadership was the only effective way to defend them.

Where two or more are gathered together, politics is inevitable, and the 1979 Southern Baptist Convention promised some spectacular political fireworks. Like immense tectonic plates, two opposing schools of Southern Baptist thought had been pressing against each other for years, slowly grinding in different directions and determined to claim the same space. The pressure built as the two sides held firm, each waiting for the other to give way.

Though he had no official duties other than serving as a messenger (the Convention term for delegate) from his church, Brother Draper was well known and respected among the denominational leaders. He was a seasoned and experienced pastor known for his success in building strong congregations and his skill as a peacemaker. His was a voice all sides of a question listened to with respect and trust, and he was well versed in the history leading up to what promised to be a historic week in Southern Baptist life: one of the great theological tectonic plates was about to move.

There were a lot of elements and chapters to the story, but one of the earliest markers of division that most everybody seemed to agree on was the publication in 1961 of *The Message of Genesis* by Dr. Ralph Elliott, a professor at Midwestern Baptist Theological Seminary in Kansas City. Despite being published by Broadman Press, a division of the Baptist Sunday School Board, the book took the position that stories in Genesis such as Noah and the Flood were not historical events. Elliott wrote that someone reading the Bible "must come to the place that he sees the parabolic and symbolic nature of much of the Old Testament Scriptures. Genesis is to be understood in this light. It is not science . . . it is impossible to deny the fact that sometimes the material may have been 'legendized' just a bit and perhaps heightened as a means of intensifying the dominant characteristics in [Noah's] life."

Elliott doubted the existence of Abraham, considered Melchizedek a priest of Baal, and summarized his approach by stating, "We must learn to think of the stories of Genesis, the creation, the fall, Noah's ark, the tower of Babel in the same way as we think of the parables of Jesus; they are profoundly symbolical (although not allegorical) stories, which aren't to be taken as literally true (like the words of a textbook of geology)."

Elliott defended his interpretation against his critics and received a vote of confidence from the Midwestern Seminary trustees. Even so, Elliott was dismissed from his teaching post the following year, but the official reason was that he and the trustees disagreed over whether to republish the book and had nothing to do with Elliott's interpretation of Scripture.

Broadman Press continued to defend the work, and the editor of the *Western Recorder* in Kentucky spoke for many pro-Elliott Baptists when he wrote, "If [Elliott] is a heretic, then he is one of many and indeed is not at the head of the line. Professors in all our seminaries know that Elliott is in the same stream of thinking with most of them, and is more in the center of the stream than some of them."

And so the battle was joined: on one side Elliott and his followers defending academic freedom to teach a variety of scriptural interpretations, and on the other his critics who claimed he was outside the boundaries of acceptable Baptist thinking. At the 1962 Southern Baptist Convention in San Francisco, a resolution was passed objecting to "the dissemination of theological views in any of our seminaries which would undermine" faith in "the historical accuracy and doctrinal integrity of the Bible." But in the years that followed there was no statement from Midwestern or any other Baptist seminary affirming that position. Many preachers and laymen opposed any challenge to scriptural inerrancy, but more and more it was this relativism of Elliott that was being taught in the seminaries.

While both camps were known by more than one name over the years, Baptists holding the traditional view that the Bible was in every way the infallible word of God eventually became recognized as "conservatives," while those who accepted some biblical accounts as parables or allegories, or otherwise challenged the conservative viewpoint, were called "moderates."

Jimmy Draper was a conservative by belief and by heritage, and was in Houston that week because, along with other conservatives, he felt they had the best chance ever to start a process that would return the denomination to its conservative roots.

Jimmy had seen reminders of the simmering conflict earlier in the week during the Pastors Conference preceding the Convention, when for the first time anyone could remember a Convention presidential candidate, Adrian Rogers, was endorsed from the platform. Jimmy was elected president of the Conference, an honor bestowed during the closing minutes of the final session upon the one who will plan the next year's event. The Conference was an unofficial prelude to the Convention, but one that often set the stage and groomed the leadership for the Convention in years to come.

Moderates, sensing momentum building on the opposing side, accused conservatives of trying to pack the Convention by renting buses for pro-conservative messengers. Lost in the argument was the fact that groups often chartered buses to the Convention and that this year it made more sense than ever: first, because hotel rooms near the convention site were in short supply; and second, because the country was in the midst of an oil crisis that had prompted President Jimmy Carter to ration gasoline.

Even the denominational media had lost its perspective. Describing the opening of the Convention, the *Baptist Standard* would report "a parade of preachers" on hand "to lead out in purging Baptist seminaries and colleges of liberalism and recommitting the Southern Baptist Convention to the belief that the Bible is the infallible, inerrant Word of God."

By the time Jimmy started on foot from his hotel to the Summit for the Convention's opening session, the thermometer was already past eighty degrees and headed north of ninety. Having grown up in Houston, he was dressed for the weather in a crisp poplin suit. The pastel shirt and stylish tie added a note of flair: Brother Draper was a firm believer that a preacher ought to look professional, but there was no reason he couldn't have a little style.

He was forty-three, a little over medium height with a trim, athletic build that reflected his lifelong love of basketball and baseball. His sandy hair, conservatively cut, had darkened with age, but there was still no hint of gray at the temples. Beside him walked his youngest brother, Charlie, twelve years his junior and also a pastor.

As they headed up the sidewalk outside Greenway Plaza toward the bank of glass doors at the main entrance to the Summit, the two caught sight of a man running toward them. It was, Charlie thought to himself, awfully hot to be running like that in a suit.

Within a couple of seconds the man stood before them, clearly agitated. It was Leon McBeth, a Baptist colleague and church historian at Southwestern Baptist Theological Seminary in Fort Worth, Jimmy's alma mater. As he took his last running step, McBeth grabbed Jimmy by both lapels and pulled him so that their faces were scarcely an inch from each other. Beads of sweat stood on his forehead, and his eyes had a look somewhere between concern and desperation.

"Don't let them destroy our Convention!" he said.

McBeth froze for an instant. Then, before either of the Drapers could respond, hurried into the convention hall.

Adrian Rogers's election would indeed be a disaster for the moderates, at least in the short term. While Jimmy had made no secret of his conservative stance, neither had he gone out of his way to broadcast it. He believed the theological fissure that had opened could be bridged more readily by looking for points of agreement between the two sides rather than points of conflict. However, when the core question came up of whether the Bible was 100 percent inerrant, Jimmy had no choice but to side with the conservatives and the man they thought had the best chance of championing their theology on a broader scale, Dr. Adrian Rogers.

Rogers, the young, telegenic, and popular pastor of the huge Bellevue Baptist Church in Memphis, was a passionate and articulate conservative that some had wanted to nominate as Convention president in previous years. Jimmy Allen, a pastor from San Antonio, actively campaigned for the post in 1977 by claiming he had to be elected to keep conservatives in general and Adrian Rogers in particular out of office. Rogers was not nominated then, and with the conservative vote split between two other candidates, Allen won the office.

Convention presidents are eligible for no more than two consecutive one-year terms, and Allen won reelection in 1978. The conservatives made a splash that year by nominating actress and recording artist Anita Bryant for first vice president. Thanks to a storm of opposition based on the fact that she was a woman (and an inexperienced one at that), she was defeated by two to one.

Though conservatives had prominent denominational positions in the past, and though resolutions of all sorts were passed endorsing the idea of scriptural inerrancy, the moderate viewpoint held sway year after year because the conservatives had no clear plan for penetrating the bureaucracy that actually held the reins of power. What happened in the months leading up to the Houston Convention was that a group of conservatives finally broke the code.

Judge Paul Pressler, an appellate court judge in Houston, was a dedicated and well-known Baptist layman who led the charge in finding out exactly how the machinery of the Southern Baptist Convention worked, and how the conservatives could turn resolutions into actions that would steer the seminaries and other entities back in a traditional direction.

The key was in the SBC president's power to appoint the Committee on Committees, which nominated members of the Committee on Boards (known today as the Committee on Nominations), which in turn nominated candidates for seminary trustees and other crucial positions. Previous presidents with conservative leanings made nominations based on recommendations from savvy, self-perpetuating moderates who made sure the levers of power remained in friendly hands.

Researching the Convention's charter and other legal documents, Pressler and his allies discovered that for the conservatives to gain ground the president had to blaze a new trail in appointing the Committee on Committees. Adrian Rogers could and would do that if elected. And so the conservatives were keen on getting him in office, and the moderates equally dedicated to keeping him out.

Jimmy Draper had friends on both sides of the equation, and he knew the moderates shuddered at the thought of a Rogers presidency. Leon McBeth had made that clear in his encounter on the street. (Draper couldn't have known then that McBeth, who was an old friend, had been to an ad hoc meeting of Southwestern Seminary faculty in town for the SBC event, where the school's president, Russell Dilday, warned that the future of

Southwestern and the Southern Baptist Convention were at stake, and that "the Convention wants to turn seminaries into Bible schools.")

At the Pastors Conference, W. A. Criswell, revered denominational leader and megachurch pastor of First Baptist in Dallas, set the tone by announcing that the upcoming SBC conclave would be great "if for no other reason than to elect Adrian Rogers as our president." There had been little other official politicking on Rogers's behalf, but behind the scenes Pressler and others strongly supported him, and his nomination gained ground rapidly by word-of-mouth.

On the Monday night before nominations would take place the next morning, Jimmy met with a group of other pastors to talk, pray, and seek the Lord's wisdom in the upcoming process. Gathering in Billy Weber's hotel room, the circle included Charlie Draper, Paige Patterson (president of Criswell Bible Institute, a longtime friend of Jimmy's, and another leading conservative), Bailey Smith (pastor of First Southern Baptist Church of Del City, Oklahoma, who had an interest himself in the presidency but had deferred to Rogers), and others.

Shortly before midnight the group broke up. On the way to their rooms, Patterson and Jerry Vines (a pastor from Mobile, Alabama, who was also considered a viable conservative candidate) encountered Adrian Rogers and his wife Joyce, returning from a late supper where they had gone to discuss the prospect of Rogers's nomination. Joyce had recommended against it, and Adrian valued her judgment highly. To Patterson's utter astonishment, Rogers told him he had changed his mind and would not allow himself to be nominated. It was, he said, "not the kind of ministry I'm called to." (Some participants have a slightly different recollection of events: that Dr. and Mrs. Rogers were intercepted on their way to dinner, told the others of their change of heart, and returned to their room to pray with Patterson and Vines.)

It was, as Charlie Draper later recalled, "a frantic ten or twelve hours" as word spread that Rogers was withdrawing. The conservatives had no formal plan for what they had done, and certainly no backup candidate. The moderates on the other hand were loaded for bear. They had a slate of candidates with rich Baptist pedigrees and planned to nominate several of them.

The most likely moderate candidate was Dr. Robert Naylor, a respected and beloved denominational leader who had retired under pressure as president of Southwestern Seminary, and whom some believed deserved the SBC presidency as just restitution. He was also as theologically conservative as many of the conservative faction, but hoped the conservative/moderate split could be healed without the Southern Baptists becoming a house divided. Bill Self, an Atlanta pastor, was squarely in the moderate camp, and felt encouragement from moderate leaders to run. Also in the hunt was Abner McCall, president of Baylor University and supporter of the cause of academic freedom that was a rallying cry in many moderate circles.

Back in his hotel room, Adrian Rogers prayed late into the night along with his wife, Patterson, and Vines. Finally, with only a few hours left before the nominating session, Joyce reversed her decision, Rogers reversed his, and Dr. Rogers's name was placed before the messengers as a candidate for president. Rogers felt it was God's will that he should run.

Tuesday the ballots were marked and collected. Judge Pressler wrote years later about a recurring dream he'd had in the days leading up to this moment, that there was a crowd of people marching down the street in Houston toward the Summit singing "We're Marching to Zion." He continued:

The time between the voting and the announcement
of the results was filled with tension. Jimmy Allen, as
president, went to the microphone and said that [regis-
tration secretary] Lee Porter was there to announce the
presidential election results. He stepped aside to let Lee
approach the microphone, but Lee was not there.
Confusion reigned on the platform. Finally, Jimmy
[Allen] called on the song leader to lead some music
while they found Lee Porter. The song leader came to
the microphone and announced that the messengers
would stand and sing the hymn, "We're Marching to
Zion." Immediately I remembered my recurring dream.
Now I knew what it meant. I knew that Adrian Rogers
had been elected president of the convention without a
runoff. . . . I collapsed crying into my seat and told
Paige [Patterson] (who was seated next to me) what
I suspected had happened.

Jimmy Draper and his wife, Carol Ann, had left the noise and
commotion of the convention floor to sit up in the stadium seats
and wait in relative quiet for the election results. As the totals
were announced Jimmy wrote on a scrap of paper, "Adrian's won
on the first ballot!" No one in either camp had expected such dramatic news.

Candidates had to get 50 percent plus one vote to be elected,
and Adrian Rogers had garnered more than 51 percent on the
first ballot. Of the five other candidates, Naylor received 23 percent of the votes and Bill Self 14 percent. The rest were in
single digits.

It was a triumph for the conservatives, but as he traveled
home to Euless, Jimmy Draper knew there was a long road still
ahead. He resolved then and there that the Pastors Conference

he planned for 1980 would be as politics-free as he could make it. This would have to be a year of healing and reaching out, of theological firmness combined with a heart for reconciliation. It was a combination of goals Brother Jimmy had plenty of experience in reaching for, and a job he would tackle with customary enthusiasm.

Young as he was, Draper had already spent twenty-three years as a pastor. It had been quite a journey so far. And it all began with two men in a small Texas town talking about a sick cow.

CHAPTER 2

$\mathcal{F}$IRST CHURCH

Dr. Howard Cargill drove up the Old San Antonio Road
headed north. A few miles in front of him was the little town
of Franklin, where his friend and client Bill Shaw waited, watching and listening for the first sign of his truck on the pavement.
Dr. Cargill spent a lot of time driving the country roads that radi-
ated out in every direction from his office in Bryan, but that was
what a veterinarian in the Texas Hill Country accepted as part of
the job.

Cargill's practice covered farmers and ranchers in east-central
Texas, roughly the middle of a triangle with Dallas, San Antonio,
and Houston as its points. The land there was drier and hillier than
the Piney Woods to the east, tamer and more lush than the desert
and mountains on the west. Quiet little settlements with distinctive
names dotted the landscape: Dime Box, Old Dime Box, North
Zulch, Round Rock, Personville, Ben Hur.

Cargill arrived at the Shaw place and, after exchanging greet-
ings with Bill, went to work on the sick animal he'd come to treat.
As the doctor went about his business, Bill stayed to keep him

company. Somehow the talk turned to church and the fact that Dr. Cargill's church in Bryan was without a pastor.

"I'll tell you somebody that deserves a look," Bill Shaw said.

"Who's that?" the doctor asked.

"Jimmy Draper. He's a real young fella, goes to Baylor. We don't have a pastor right now either, and Brother Jimmy came to preach for us here in Franklin last week. He did a heck of a job. If you're looking to call a pastor, he's worth talking to."

The conversation turned to other things, but driving twenty-odd miles back to Bryan later on, Dr. Cargill thought more about young Jimmy Draper. And the more he thought, the more he figured it was worth it to meet him.

After he talked it over with some other members of the church, they extended an invitation to preach. One Sunday morning soon afterward Draper and his wife, Carol Ann, arrived at Saints Rest Baptist Church in the Steep Hollow community of Bryan after an eighty-five-mile drive from Baylor in their vintage jalopy, "Herschel." At first glance it looked like the preacher's car might be older than the preacher. Jimmy was two months shy of his twenty-first birthday and appeared even younger. He had neatly groomed hair in the style of the 1950s, trimmed around the ears with a barber's razor then longer on top and parted on the side; his boyish face was centered by a wide grin. Carol Ann was eighteen; they had been married three weeks. Busy as he was as a college student and newlywed, the hope of a permanent pulpit was enough to make him consider taking on even more responsibilities.

Saints Rest was a congregation of eighty to one hundred people that met in an old white frame church building where steam radiators clanked and hissed under the windows in cold weather and ceiling fans hummed and clattered overhead throughout the long Texas summers. Before morning worship each week, Sunday school classes convened simultaneously in the four corners of the room, with each class taking a block of seats and each teacher standing to face them or sitting sidesaddle and talking over the back of his chair. (One teacher's neck problems meant she had to sit straight in her chair, facing the same direction as her class and them watching the back of her head.)

Young or not, Brother Jimmy preached a sermon that made an impact on everyone who heard it. His gestures were confident but not grandiose, his cadences firm, pleasant, and compelling. There was a depth to the teaching and a confidence to the delivery seldom associated with a college boy. He was young enough to be the son—or the grandson—of a number of the members, but nobody seemed to mind. They were a small church without a pastor, and here was an obviously gifted young preacher looking for his first pastorate. He was a clear thinker, in command of a good voice, and left no doubt about his passion for Christ and ministry.

After the service and a hearty Sunday dinner, Jimmy and Carol Ann climbed back into Herschel for the return drive to Waco while the church considered its next step. In fact there was no real considering to do. Saints Rest had no pulpit committee to sift through résumés, no formal selection process. The church agreed by acclamation that they'd like to have Brother Jimmy if he would take the job.

Dr. Cargill's father, George, was a leading member of the church who had taught Sunday school there since before Jimmy was born. The members asked him to get in touch with Draper and make him an offer on the church's behalf. Within a day or two a telegram arrived from Bryan at the Draper apartment in Waco reading simply, "CALL UNANIMOUS. DETAILS TO FOLLOW."

The details never did follow, but Brother Draper accepted the call anyway. He had been preaching since he was fourteen, and had known every day during those years that pastoring would be his life. His course of study at Baylor was preparing him for the intellectual challenges of a seminary education; now his pastorate at Saints Rest would give him his first practical experience as a spiritual mentor.

A knotty conflict between two respected lay leaders in the congregation gave him his first test—one of those cases where the original problem could have been handled easily, but was instead allowed to fester to the point where it became a stumbling block for both parties.

The Drapers had scarcely moved to town before Jimmy got an earful of the situation and about George Cargill's part in it. In more than twenty-five years as a Sunday school teacher, George had faithfully followed the lesson outlines published by the Baptist Sunday School Board. For many of those years, Esker Martin, a fellow deacon, was a member of his class. One Sunday, teaching in his corner of the church in Steep Hollow, George discussed a lesson that had to do with prison. Esker's grandson was in prison at the time, and this somehow gave him the idea that George was singling his family out as an example. Esker took offense at what George said, but wouldn't talk about it with him. George had no idea why Esker was mad, Esker refused to say, and there the matter stood.

Regardless of the fact that either man was old enough to be his grandfather, and despite being new to the congregation and community, Brother Jimmy began looking for some way to persuade Esker to talk and for the two men to be reconciled. As a young man who favored action, honesty, and putting the past behind him, he soon went to work.

Jimmy went to Esker's house to discuss the matter. Mrs. Martin told Jimmy that Esker was out in the field on his tractor. Jimmy walked out to the field and flagged Esker down. The two of them talked, and Esker explained why he was so upset with George.

"Would you tell that to George? Right now?" Jimmy asked.

"Yes I would," the farmer answered.

"I'll be right back."

Jimmy picked up the chairman of the deacons and together they picked up George Cargill and brought him back to the Martin house. Esker explained his feelings to George, who was relieved beyond words to know at last what had upset his old friend so deeply. George in turn apologized and asked Esker's forgiveness. It was a sweet moment for Brother Jimmy as he watched the two old saints, their eyes brimming with tears, hugging each other in a renewal of their longstanding Christian brotherhood.

By the time he received his bachelor's degree from Baylor in the spring of 1957, Jimmy had been the pastor of the Steep Hollow congregation for almost a year. In January he began supplementing his modest salary working Saturdays at Waldrup's men's clothing store in Bryan. After he graduated, he worked there full-time, joining the ranks of thousands of bi-vocational Baptist pastors across the country. During Jimmy's senior year he drove back and forth countless times between attending college in Waco and preaching in Bryan; now it was a relief to be in one place for a while.

Home was now a two-bedroom parsonage the church provided in Steep Hollow, a humble place that Carol Ann considered "sparse but comfortable." She had been out of high school only three months when she got married; married just over a month when Jimmy took his first church in Bryan; married less than six months when she learned recently that their first child was on the way. In scarcely a year she had gone from high school senior to pastor's wife and mother-to-be.

Life had been something of a whirlwind for Carol Ann Floyd Draper ever since she met Jimmy at church back home in Lake Jackson. It was all the more astonishing because she had known for years that the last thing on earth she wanted to be was a pastor's wife.

Lake Jackson was 150 miles and a world away from Bryan, and even more removed from the rural community of Steep Hollow. A small town in itself, Lake Jackson had a big-city tempo, anchoring a teeming area between Houston—then a city of 400,000—and the beaches of Freeport and Surfside on the Gulf of Mexico south of Galveston.

Carol Ann had gone to First Baptist Church of Lake Jackson as long as she could remember. When she was only seven, she sensed the special and unmistakable presence of Jesus in her heart: she was saved by His sacrifice. As her family looked on with prayers of thanksgiving, she was baptized as a public expression of her faith and her belief in Christ as the one and only Savior.

Two years later she surrendered her life for special service, making a vow to devote her life and career to spreading the gospel in whatever way the Lord would guide her. She thought she might get a teaching degree, then become a missionary, serving Christ in some distant corner of the world. Another possibility was working with Wycliffe Bible Translators. Named in honor of the fourteenth-century scholar who first published the Scriptures in English, the Wycliffe organization translated the Bible into obscure languages in remote areas, often in places where a written language was unknown and had to be developed from scratch.

In the summer of 1955, Carol Ann Floyd was a rising senior at Lake Jackson High, head majorette, and an active member of her youth group at church. In August she went to a revival with her family and friends. She sang in the revival choir, and she couldn't help taking special notice of the guest song leader. He seemed so full of energy, and even from the platform he projected a sense of conviction and genuineness she found appealing. His name was Jimmy Draper. He had gone to high school in Houston but was now getting ready to start his third year at Baylor.

Jimmy had a fine singing voice, and knew that music was an important part of any revival. There were people who felt the presence of God moving in them for the first time through music. The singing and the message in the lyrics added to the sense of celebration and joy that was an essential part of the revival experience. Jimmy had conducted team revivals in the past, singing one night and preaching the next. He'd actually had this weekend off, but there was a last-minute change in plans. So there he stood with his wide smile and strong tenor voice, a magnet for admiring glances from the girls.

Carol Ann's pastor thought she and Jimmy might enjoy knowing each other, and introduced them. There was something more to him, she thought, than being a gregarious and gifted revivalist. The best word she could think of to describe it was *spiritual*. She was attracted by his spirit of dedication to his work that came through loud and clear in his music, in his speaking, and in his prayers. There was a spark she couldn't identify exactly; somehow, in some way she couldn't exactly explain, the Lord had a special hold on Jimmy's heart.

The two got to know each other that weekend, each remaining in the other's thoughts long after the last notes of revival music died away. After the school year started, Jimmy wrote

Carol Ann from college, and she wrote him back. Their friendship grew through their letters, interspersed with occasional visits on the rare weekends when Jimmy wasn't preaching or leading a revival somewhere. She began to realize how deeply he loved the Lord. She realized too that she was beginning to love him.

Finally one day she prayed, "Lord, I'm falling in love with Jimmy Draper. And Lord, You know I'm not pastor's wife material–I'm a twirler in the band!"

Carol Ann began talking to her parents about the prospect of marriage. Her mother was quick to point out that neither one of them had a job. How would they support themselves? One way or another, Carol Ann knew, the Lord would provide for her and her husband. She had fallen in love by faith; now she was prepared to begin her married life trusting in God to take care of their daily needs. While pastoring a small church didn't pay much, she and Jimmy didn't need much: they had each other and a world of God-given opportunity.

Carol Ann graduated from high school in May 1956, and she and Jimmy were married in Lake Jackson in July. The newlyweds headed for the Baylor campus in Waco. When Jimmy accepted the call at Steep Hollow, Carol Ann resolved to find a place as soon as possible where she could serve in the church. It seemed to her that most pastors' wives played the piano, but she had steadfastly refused her mother's suggestion to practice and never learned to play very well. After all, she'd had no intention of becoming a pastor's wife.

Struggling with self-doubt and wondering how she could possibly help her husband in his first pastorate, she prayed that the church would ask her to do something she could do. Members invited her to organize the Vacation Bible School for the next summer. The pastor had always been the principal of VBS in the past, but he couldn't do it because he was still working at Waldrup's that first year of his pastorate. Even though Carol Ann was inexperienced and unsure of her ability—she had never even taught Bible school, much less been the principal—she agreed to take on the task. Her attention to detail, love for the children, and shining example of cooperation brought the program to new heights of success.

To master her feelings of inadequacy she learned not to compare herself with others, and encouraged her friends and coworkers to do the same. She felt God had prepared her for this position, and He would give her whatever resources she needed to fill it to His glory. Success wasn't measured by how she performed a specific task compared with somebody else, but by how fully she used her abilities and how completely she devoted herself to serving Christ and His people.

Carol Ann found a lot of comfort in that point of view. She settled into the modest parsonage in Steep Hollow, working on her limited budget to prepare it for the arrival of their first child, due in September of 1957.

The new little Draper would be born into a family rich with history and faithful to its tradition of service in Baptist churches. In fact, there had been Drapers in the ministry for three generations and in the United States since colonial days, when a man's faith could land him in prison.

CHAPTER 3

ARKANSAS TRAVELERS

ARKANSAS, WHERE JIMMY WAS BORN, was home to four generations of Drapers, but the family traced its history back cen-
turies before that. According to *A Survey of London,* published in
1603, Sir Christopher Draper may have been one of a group of
"Marchant taylors" that established a "notable free schoole for
poore mens children" in 1560. Six years later he served as lord
mayor of London. But by then Jimmy's branch of the family had
departed for opportunities of another kind.

No one recorded the reason why, sometime before 1650,
James Draper and his wife Miriam Stansfield Draper decided to
leave a comfortable, predictable life behind and sail to the New
World. James's ancestors had lived along Draper's Lane in the village of Heptonstall, Yorkshire, in windswept northern England
since at least 1415. But as other Puritan families had done for a
generation, they braved a long, hazardous, and miserable sea
voyage–eight weeks was typical for a westbound crossing–to
live in America. James settled in Roxbury, Massachusetts, and

established himself as a weaver and cloth merchant (his name derived from the French *drapier,* a purveyor of cloth).

In Roxbury the family attended the church of John Eliot, legendary Puritan minister and missionary to the Indians, who translated the Bible into the Algonquin language as *Up-Biblium God,* published in 1663. The friendship between the Draper and Eliot families led in time to marriages, with later Draper descendants being related by blood to Charles William Eliot, president of Harvard for more than forty years; Jared Eliot, Connecticut clergyman and personal friend of Benjamin Franklin; and other Eliot notables.

By all accounts James and Miriam lived a good life. They had eight children over twenty years (their first child had died in infancy in England), their business prospered, and James lived to what was then the remarkably advanced age of seventy-six. Three of James Draper's great-grandsons fought in the American Revolution. Moses fought in the Battle of Lexington; Samuel was a captain in the Continental Army; and Jonathan was an officer who served with the Minutemen at Lexington.

It was Jonathan who revived the long-dormant family wanderlust by leaving Roxbury in the 1780s. He and his wife, Silence Copeland Draper, moved to Vermont, on to New Hampshire, then west to Michigan; back east to New York, and finally west again, to Ohio. He died there at the age of ninety-eight.

Of their nine children, the second child, Luke, made the liveliest mark on history. Born either in Vermont or New Hampshire, Luke was a father at eighteen, and shortly thereafter abandoned his wife and young son to move to Buffalo, New York. There he was taken prisoner twice by the British during the War of 1812. He married again in 1813 and lived for some time in Lockport,

New York, before moving to Toledo, Ohio, where he was eventually appointed associate county judge.

Albert, the son Luke Draper left behind, was raised by two of his mother's brothers. When he was in his early twenties he traveled east with them, where the three got jobs helping build the Erie Canal. Later they went to work on a canal in Indiana, and Albert built the first bridge across the Wabash River in Huntington County. By his own admission, Albert had "an iron constitution" that enabled him to succeed as a builder, but years of driving himself in the disease-infested creeks and marshes where the canals were built caused his health to fail. Though he had put great effort into his first career, he seemed to give it up without complaint, writing simply, "I found I must take a different course."

By 1850 Albert Draper was married and the father of six, a prosperous farmer, a justice of the peace, and a county commissioner. It must have been quite a surprise to receive, out of the blue, a letter from Lyman C. Draper, oldest of the four half brothers he had never met, asking after his welfare. Raised principally by an uncle named Jonathan (whom he knew as "Grandfather"), Albert had no knowledge of his father or his extended family.

On February 9, 1851, Albert wrote to his brother, ". . . There is much that I should like to say to you, but our relationship is of such a nature, that I know not where to begin or what to say. I will first say, that my education is so limited, that I seldom write to any person, even my best friends or relatives; but this is a favor that I never expected to enjoy. . . . You say that you some expect to pass through this region next summer, & would like to call on me, if it would be agreeable to me. I assure you there are but few things, if any, that could give me more pleasure than to receive a visit from you or any of your family. . . ."

This newfound connection also allowed Albert to track down his father in Toledo and write him for the first time ever. Though Albert was delighted beyond words to find him, the older man clearly had no interest in being found.

On March 6, 1851, Luke Draper wrote his son:

your Dockament & Bill of perticulors of Feb. the 22d Came to hand, and with all of your Researches and toilling I think you have failled to Make out a case in question. in the first place their was Never anny admittence [of paternity] on My part. Nor was there even anny testamoney against Me under Oath, and why should you assume aneything of the kind. you mite with just as mouch propriety Assume queen victory [Queen Victoria] as your half Sister. She is of good Charicter & has struggled hard to git through this world thus far and is said to bee the Mother of several Children. I have known people to make a good Living and sometimes git quite wealthy by minding their own business, supposing you practice it hereafter. from your father Luke Draper

However Albert felt about his father's rejection, he provided his own children with a good home and a reputation of high esteem in the community. On April 4, 1858, he and his wife were both baptized and joined the Rockcreek Township Baptist Church of Huntington County, the first members of the Draper clan known to be Baptists. According to one contemporary account, Draper had "a fine property, first rate farm, and is a first rate man. . . . He married well and has a promising family."

Albert's son Benjamin Franklin Draper was the first of the family to live in Arkansas. When he married his wife, Sarah, they lived in Alton, Illinois, just across the Mississippi River from

St. Louis on some of the richest river-bottom farm land in the world. He began truck farming on a large scale and was soon renowned in the region for his "high class melons, berries, and vegetables." After a time, Sarah developed arthritis so severe that Ben left his successful enterprise and moved the family to Hot Spring County, Arkansas, where the mineral baths were widely recommended for a range of illnesses. At first they lived in Malvern, just southeast of Hot Springs, fifty miles from Little Rock on the road to Texarkana. Their home was atop a bluff on the edge of town still known today as Draper's Ridge—a historic echo of Draper's Lane in far-off Yorkshire.

After a time Ben moved his family six miles to the community of Gifford, where the watermelons raised on his forty acres there became legendary; family tradition holds that he harvested the first melons in Arkansas every year. Like his parents, Benjamin was a devout Baptist, and became a senior lay leader of the Baptist church in Malvern. His wife, by contrast, was a Methodist. Since neither wanted to give up long-held beliefs, the two went to separate churches every Sunday.

Ben was a mainstay of his congregation, and even as a layman had a deep concern for the spiritual welfare of friends and family. Asked to pray at one particular family gathering, he went on and on until he felt the room growing impatient, then jovially ended with, "I get you all together so seldom I have to make the most of it. Amen."

His popularity made it all the more tragic when his neighbors heard through the grapevine—and read later in the local newspaper—that eighty-two-year-old Mr. Draper had been killed fighting a fire on his farm. Under the headline, "Hot Spring County Pioneer Meets Horrible Death," the story reported Draper's body was discovered tangled in a fence near the blaze, the rake he presumably used to beat the flames lying nearby. It was unclear whether he died from exhaustion or smoke inhalation. The account praised Draper as "one of Malvern's pioneer citizens" and "one of our most progressive farmers."

In assessing Benjamin Franklin Draper's contribution to the region, the reporter continued: "He was always active in church work and was well versed in the Bible, following its teachings to the letter. Not only was he deeply religious but took a very keen interest in politics, keeping well informed on everything in national and state matters, his opinion being respected by both his own party and those who differed with him in these matters. He was a man among men and at his going Hot Spring County loses one of her best citizens, and one whose influence for good will remain although he has gone on to a better land, and his friendship remembered by all as one of their fondest memories."

There were six active pallbearers at the funeral and eleven honorary ones, including a congressman, a judge, and two doctors: a prominent collection of men for so small a community—yet another indication of the regard county residents had for their late "pioneer citizen." The pastor of First Baptist Church, Malvern, was Reverend Leonard Marcellus Keeling, for many years a friend of the Draper family. No doubt he conducted the service while feeling a mixture of sadness at the loss and thanksgiving for so long and exemplary a life.

Less than five years after Reverend Keeling officiated at that funeral service for his friend Ben Draper in the summer of 1929, his daughter Lois Jeanne married Ben's grandson James Thomas. The Keeling family had a pedigree as rich and ancient as the Drapers, tracing its line back as far as 1216, when one John Killing held the local office of provost in County Dorset, England (one source says the family originated that year in County Stafford,

Ireland). The Arkansas Keelings were probably direct descendants of Thomas Keeling, who arrived in America about 1635 and settled in Norfolk County, Virginia, where he served as church warden, justice, and lieutenant in the militia.

Leonard Moses Keeling, the first of the family to live in Arkansas, arrived in Nevada County some time shortly after the Civil War. Leonard Marcellus was the second of three children born to Moses' son Joseph Washington Keeling. When Leonard Marcellus was eighteen months old and his older sister Regina was three, their mother died a day after giving birth to their sister Mattie.

The three children went to live with their aunt and uncle on a farm, and it was there, at age seventeen, that Leonard Marcellus first claimed Christ as his Savior. He continued with his farming for the time being, but soon after his marriage to Nancy Pearl Compton in 1902 he felt God calling him to full-time ministry. He was hesitant to make the change because he thought he lacked the education ministers needed. But his brother-in-law advised, "If God called you to preach, you don't need an education because God will put the words to say in your mouth."

With only his faith in the calling to guide him, and with the support of his wife, Keeling began preaching at little country churches in the area. His pay was usually in kind—a chicken or a sack of potatoes. After a few years Nancy, a school teacher who saw the value of formal education, told him that if he was going to preach, he ought to be the best preacher out there, and that meant getting an education.

Following a season of prayer, Keeling took his wife's advice, attending Ouachita Baptist College in Arkadelphia, Arkansas, while pastoring a church in nearby Prescott. After graduation in 1909 he moved his family to Fort Worth, Texas, where he studied at Southwestern Baptist Seminary, pastoring in the nearby towns of Coolidge and Irving until earning his degree in 1912. Just before returning to Arkansas after graduation, Nancy gave birth to their fifth child, Lois Jeanne, in Coolidge on January 10, 1912.

When she was ten months old, Lois Draper contracted polio. It left her unable to walk normally. For the first fifteen years of her life, her mobility often was restricted, and she endured more than a dozen surgeries on one of her legs in unsuccessful efforts to repair the damage.

In a final effort to allow her to walk, using such primitive medical science and surgical techniques as were available at the time, the doctors broke bones in her foot and ankle in such a way that they would all fuse together. The leg ended up several inches shorter and the foot two sizes smaller, and so radical a solution left her with a stiff, peg-leg gait. But for the first time in her life she could walk unassisted.

By the time the family moved to Malvern in 1926 there were three more siblings to ride herd on, making eight children in all around the Keeling table every mealtime. They were never a wealthy family; in some years Brother Keeling didn't have a car and carried on his extensive round of pastoral visitations on foot or horseback. But they were a happy family. Lois never remembered a cross word between her parents, and she often heard her father rise before daybreak to pray.

It was only natural for the Keelings and Drapers to spend a lot of time together. Old Benjamin had six children and a host of grandchildren, many of whom were faithful members of First Baptist in Malvern. His third child, William, had six children of his own, the youngest being James Thomas Draper, born August 26, 1913.

William had a good job with the railroad and was a respon-sible provider. But tragedy befell the family when his wife, Lillian May Poff Draper, died in January, 1914. Baby James was not yet six months old; the oldest child, named Lillian May after her mother, was only ten. Railroading was the only work William knew, and he found it impossible to raise the children on his own. No one, it seemed, could take on the responsibility of all six, and so over time they were parceled out to different families.

Lillian went to live with the Butler family in Leola, Arkansas. The next four children in age, Lucille, William, Jr., Benjamin, and Rose, eventually went to Denver to live with their maiden mater-nal aunt Rose Poff, a public school teacher. Rose and Ben went first, soon after their mother's death; Lucille followed in 1916 and Ben Jr. a year later. James was taken in by Mr. and Mrs. Frederick Macomber, faithful neighbors of the Drapers who lived in Leola.

William did what he could to keep in touch with his scattered family, but he himself died when little Jimmie was only seven. Frederick Macomber died two years afterward, leaving Jimmie in the care of Mrs. Macomber and her daughter, who had moved back home following a failed marriage.

And so it was when Lois Keeling met Jimmie Draper, he was something of an orphan, though the Macomber ladies were devoted to him and he wrote often to his siblings and Aunt Rose in Denver. Once in 1926 he took the train from Malvern to Denver by himself to visit Rose and his four siblings. He kept a diary, which he called his "Memoranda Book" and dedicated to "Mrs. J. F. Macomber, my loving foster-mother."

Jimmie also had loved his grandfather Ben very much. One story the family often told in later years was that the day he surrendered to preach, he and a friend started out riding their bicycles to Grandfather's to tell him the news. The boys got tired and turned back, planning to leave earlier the next morning. But that day, before they could make their second trip, Grandfather died in the fire.

The Macombers were Methodists, so despite his Baptist heritage Jimmie received his early Christian teaching at the Methodist church in Malvern. He also went to the Methodist church with Aunt Rose when he visited her out west. He loved playing tennis, and was always ready for a pick-up game. Jimmie also enjoyed reading and spent lots of time at the public library, especially in the summer. Pastor Keeling had one of the largest private libraries in town, more than two thousand volumes, and no doubt Jimmie had his choice of that collection as well.

In addition to the influence of the Draper family's Baptist tradition, Jimmie was drawn back to the Baptist church by a growing attraction to Lois Keeling. By the time he graduated from high school, he and Lois Keeling had fallen in love. They were married July 24, 1934, with Dr. Keeling officiating; Lois was twenty-two, James a month under twenty. Like his new father-in-law, James soon felt the call to preach and enrolled in Ouachita Baptist College, as Dr. Keeling had, to prepare for seminary. Receiving his degree there, he also followed Keeling in attending Southwestern Seminary in Fort Worth.

In the tradition of so many seminarians, James pastored a church while working toward his degree, traveling back and forth each week from church to campus in order to generate some badly needed income. He had two small churches in Arkansas, and the logistics and expense of ping-ponging from there to Fort Worth every week were a real challenge. A thoughtful and generous benefactor came to the rescue in Senator D. D. Glover, a member of First Baptist Malvern who, with a senator's connections, secured a pair of railroad passes for the young couple that allowed them to ride between Arkansas and Fort Worth indefinitely for free.

By the spring of 1935, James and Lois were expecting their first child, but Lois continued accompanying her husband on his weekly train excursions for as long as she could. When the big event finally occurred, it happened so fast there was no time to get to the hospital. And so to everyone's surprise, the Drapers' first child, a son, was born at home in Hartford, Arkansas, on the morning of October 10, 1935. They named him James Thomas Draper, Jr., in honor of his father, and perhaps with a nod as well to the ancestral James who had been brave and adventurous enough to leave his comfortable life and business in Yorkshire to stake a claim in the New World.

CHAPTER 4

THE CALL

LITTLE JIMMY'S EARLIEST MEMORIES revolved around church life. When his parents lived in Fort Worth while his father finished his seminary studies, the family lived in a four-unit apartment complex. One of their neighbors was Anne Margrett, granddaughter of the Bagby family, the first Baptist missionaries in Brazil, and the widow of an English businessman who had lived in Argentina. She later spent many years in Argentina as a missionary herself. She had a daughter, Doreen, about the same age as the Drapers' son, and the two children were frequent playmates. Jimmy enjoyed listening to Mrs. Margrett's stories of real-life jungle adventures and sharing the story of Jesus with people whose world was unimaginably different from the one he knew.

His daddy preached in Arkansas every weekend, and by now had a half-time pastorate in the town of Forester. It was a small church in a small community, where there was no monthly budget for a pastor's salary. His pay consisted of the money in the offering plate, which one of the deacons emptied into a paper sack after the service and gave him to take home. After he got back to the seminary, his wife and son would gather around as he emptied the sack onto the bed and counted the coins and occasional dollar bills.

Some weeks were relatively rewarding and others lean by comparison, so the final count was always a big family event. Little Jimmy picked up on the excitement of the moment enough so that, when someone asked him, "Why does your daddy preach?" he could answer with confidence, "For the money!"

Vacations were economical but fun-filled trips to visit relatives. Jimmy's mother cheerfully managed all the packing and traveling, even though in the 1930s and 1940s physical disability was a far greater barrier to getting around in public than it was in later years. Because five aunts and two uncles were living out west, there were always adventures waiting in that direction. One year when he was about four, Jimmy came down with the whooping cough on the way to visit family in Albuquerque. By the time the family got to their destination Jimmy's dad had it too; before long he had passed it on to their hosts, making it a red-letter event in family lore as the "summer Jimmy gave everybody the whooping cough."

When he was five, Jimmy's family moved to Clarksville, Arkansas, where his father took a full-time pastorate and Jimmy enrolled in the public school in September 1941. World War II was beginning its third brutal year in Europe, and the economy was just completing a long, slow recovery from the Great Depression. But life in a small river town in the Ozark foothills was relatively quiet and fulfilling. Clarksville was a modest, unassuming place where doors were seldom locked and everybody knew your name.

The same year Jimmy helped welcome a new brother, George, into the family. Even as a first grader Jimmy felt a sense of responsibility for his new baby brother. When George got old enough to walk, Jimmy was often the one who watched him, played with him, and dashed after him when his mother's limited mobility kept her from being two or three places at once, the way she wished she could.

In one memorable episode when he was three or so, George overheard his parents talking about someone who was in the hospital. Since Daddy visited people in the hospital, George decided he would too. He walked from home, crossed a busy railroad track, and appeared at the hospital, where the astonished volunteer receptionist called Brother Draper to come and get his independent-minded son.

A life-changing event took place in young Jimmy's life during the family's time in Clarksville, though it happened in another town nearby. It was the moment Jimmy felt Christ in his heart, and knew beyond any doubt he was saved by the blood of Jesus.

His father was preaching a revival one night and Jimmy, as usual, was there to listen with his mother and baby George. He had been in church several times a week for as long as he could remember. He had listened as his daddy read the Bible out loud at home every night, and as he prayed for God's mercy on his family. Jimmy knew by heart the story of Jesus, the world's only perfect human, and how by dying He took on the sins of the world so that others might be saved from the punishment they rightly deserved. None of us could earn God's favor on our own, he learned, but any of us could believe Jesus died for us, saved us from the consequences of our sin, and paid our way to eternal life in heaven.

Perhaps all the pieces weren't quite in place in his young heart, but the assurance of salvation definitely was. And so when his daddy invited all who would be saved to claim Jesus as Savior, Jimmy made that claim inside. It was a wonderful feeling.

Within two years of their move to Clarksville, Brother Draper answered a call to preach in far-off Bay City, Texas. America by then was in the midst of a two-front war, fighting Japan in the Pacific and Germany in Europe. Coastal Texas had become one of the nation's most important oil refining centers. As production of aviation fuel, gasoline, and other war supplies multiplied, workers flocked to the area. Along with growth of every other kind, churches increased their attendance, and new churches were formed to serve the spiritual needs of the newcomers.

First Baptist Church Bay City was twenty miles or so inland in a relatively undeveloped area between the ports of Galveston and Port Lavaca, south of the busiest area of new growth. In some ways it must have seemed an alien world to a native Arkansan: hot, humid, dotted with scrub cedar and stunted live oaks, and flat as a tabletop compared to the cool, rich, green mountain foothills where Brother Draper had so recently served, and where the clear-running Arkansas River wound its way through the rolling countryside.

Though the family didn't stay long in Bay City, young Jimmy took another important step in his Christian walk. It was there that he made a public profession of faith and was baptized. The assurance of his salvation had become a part of his life, and he wanted to share it more fully with everyone he knew. There was no better way to do it than to make his faith public, then take the historic Baptist step of believer's baptism by immersion.

With the close of the war came the end of emergency-level petroleum production, and the population of the Texas coast underwent another change. In 1945 Brother Draper left Bay City, but not to return all the way to Arkansas. Rather he accepted a call from Central Baptist Church, about half the way back in Jacksonville, surrounded by the lush pine forests of East Texas.

It was a good place to grow up. Jimmy started the fourth grade there and soon had a whole neighborhood full of friends. There was a radio in the house for Jimmy to listen to, but most of the fun Jimmy had was whatever adventures he and his buddies came up with on their own. As he got older Jimmy also steadily took on more responsibility. When he was twelve and George was six, another brother, Charlie, was born. Between preaching revivals and visiting people in the community, Brother Draper was away from home much of the time. With three children at home, Jimmy became ever more important to his mother in running the household and looking after the younger boys.

Together with the effects of polio, Lois Draper also suffered from arthritis, further limiting what she could do and increasing her dependence on Jimmy. They tackled household chores as a team. Mother could mop the floor if Jimmy would wring out the mop for her; she could churn fresh butter if he would take a turn at the dasher. Churning was one job Jimmy did willingly; he remembered the tasteless margarine of wartime rationing, stark white and packed with liquid yellow coloring to drizzle on and mix in. Homemade butter was well worth the trouble.

His daddy's health was delicate too by this time, though James Draper was only in his mid-30s. Back in Bay City, little Jimmy had watched him play tennis, a sport his father had enjoyed since before he was a teenager. Now he had to be more conscious of overexertion, and his doctor suggested he start playing golf instead of tennis because it was easier on his heart. Brother Draper started playing at the local club, and Jimmy caddied for him. It wasn't long until young Jimmy cultivated a love for the game and was playing himself, using balls he rooted out of the roughs and fished out of water hazards. If he didn't find any balls, he couldn't play, and so he became an expert ball spotter.

Team sports appealed to Jimmy too, and he played them all. In the 1940s high school sports seasons never overlapped. That made it possible to go out for football in the fall, basketball in winter, and baseball and track in the spring. Jimmy could practice sports until dark, then walk home for dinner, sometimes stopping for a quart of milk to drink on the way home. When there was no practice at school, Jimmy and his friends played pick-up football, or made their own high jump in somebody's back yard. He became a skilled and enthusiastic three-season athlete, yet remained ever mindful of his mother's needs around the house. At fourteen he got a hardship driver's license so he could do household errands and pick up his brothers from school or the babysitter.

Sunday was an island of quiet in those busy weeks. Of course the mornings were reserved for church activities. After Sunday lunch at home there was a family quiet time that was ideal for taking a nap. After that, Jimmy and his friends played outside until church services in the evening.

Every summer during the contented family years when Jimmy was growing up, the Drapers went to family camp at Piney Woods Encampment, deep in the forests of East Texas. One night after hearing a sermon and invitation by Dr. Boyd Hunt in the gymnasium, Jimmy felt God calling him to do something special. As he had known when he was saved, and again when he was baptized, he knew the Lord was guiding him toward something new, some higher level of commitment. This time the goal was not as clear. He walked forward during the invitation and said he was rededicating himself to Christ. To himself he added, *I just don't know exactly how.*

It took two more years before Jimmy learned "exactly how" the Lord had in mind to use him. It was the summer of 1950, and Jimmy was fourteen. In the years since World War II, revival meetings had claimed a prominent place in American Evangelical worship. The revival service had been a mainstay of outreach off and on for generations: a series of preaching services held nightly for a week (some lasted longer, some were shorter), featuring music, testimonies, evangelistic preaching, and ending with an invitation for listeners to make professions of faith, be baptized, dedicate their lives to missionary work or other special service, or otherwise express publicly their faith in Christ and their assurance of salvation.

In the summer of 1949, a young Wheaton College graduate from North Carolina named Billy Graham had pitched a tent in downtown Los Angeles, sent his associate Cliff Barrows to warm up the audience with his trombone, and preached the message that the city needed a spiritual revival; that the solution to the problems of modern life was in the teachings of Jesus Christ; that inviting Christ into your heart was the key to joy and fulfillment. The Los Angeles event, scheduled to run a week, ran a solid month instead. By the time it was over, Billy Graham was a national figure; the next year he launched the Billy Graham Evangelistic Association.

While Graham's Los Angeles tent meetings were surely the country's best-known events of their type, students at Baylor University had been preaching in tents even earlier. Members of the campus Ministerial Alliance pitched a tent on a vacant lot and started proclaiming the gospel. Thousands attended, with hundreds of them professing new faith in Christ. Leading the development of the tent meetings at Baylor were young war veterans who, even in their twenties, had a worldly seriousness that drew them to the calling of evangelism.

Soon the Baptist General Convention of Texas institutionalized these student-run events as "youth led revivals," and they became popular across the state. On August 26, 1950, a youth led revival was in full swing at Brother Draper's Central Baptist Church in Jacksonville. There were two young preachers there that night named Bailey Stone and Buckner Fanning. Moved by the message, the music, and the moment, Jimmy was praying for a friend of his when he suddenly felt God responding to him in a completely unexpected way.

He sensed that God was challenging him to complete the part of his spiritual journey he had started two years before at Piney Woods: "How can I answer your prayer if you're not willing to do what I want you to do?" he heard God asking.

Jimmy felt an excitement inside unlike anything he had ever before experienced. He had gone forward for "rededications" several times in the past two years, but still hadn't been able to see which direction this spiritual pull was leading. Now suddenly it was like the fog had been blown away to clearly reveal what God wanted him to do. It was a spiritual high point that transformed his life.

He stepped forward with confidence, walked to the front of the crowd, and surrendered his life to be a preacher. Recalling the moment years later, he said, "It's a mystical thing, like being saved. You feel God calling you to something different from the secular world, something of a spiritual nature. Baptists have a sense of God calling you; it's a plan God has for your life, not a vocational choice you make. I surrendered any right I had to be anything else and vowed to devote myself to the work of the Lord."

The preachers invited him to say something. He didn't have anything planned but spoke from the heart. "I don't want anybody to feel sorry for me. This is one of the happiest moments of my life." It wasn't as if God had taken anything away from him or limited his opportunities; God had opened up a world of opportunity and promise more vast than he could ever have imagined five minutes earlier.

His father surely was pleased beyond words. It was Brother Draper's thirty-seventh birthday. One deacon teased young Jimmy after the service, "If God can call you to preach, He can do anything!"

A friend of Jimmy's, Medford Hutson, surrendered to preach the same night, and that friend got Jimmy his first preaching assignment the next weekend, which was Labor Day weekend, in Mixon, Texas. He preached a message based on sermons by George W. Truett, Charlie Matthews, and others. He had practiced and honed it to take thirty minutes. In his excitement, standing in the pulpit for the first time ever, he delivered it in twelve minutes. However his message affected the congregation that warm Texas summer night, the experience cemented the calling in his mind and heart. With the popularity of youth-led revivals at a high pitch, it wasn't long before Jimmy had other invitations to preach.

Word got around quickly in Jacksonville about Jimmy's new-found vocational commitment. During football practice the next week, one of the players swore. In the past no one would have given it a thought, but this time the coach said, "That wasn't nice, was it, Draper?"

"No, coach, it wasn't," he answered, without any further comment. As one called to preach Jimmy saw the world differently; it was obvious that the world saw him differently as well.

One friend asked him, "Are you doing it for the money?" That had to cause a chuckle in the Draper household. Maybe revival money was a good income for a high school job, but members of the Draper family well knew that preaching was not a likely path to financial security.

His dedication to preaching made him more mindful of hurtful things in the world that he saw but couldn't do anything about. One example in particular stood out in later years. In Jacksonville during the 1950s, girls sang and boys didn't–boys played football. Boys with any interest in singing were hounded mercilessly out of it by their peers. However, in spite of the long odds, there was one friend of Jimmy's who had a beautiful voice and loved to sing. He was brave enough to perform one day in the school auditorium, but before he sang more than a few notes he was hooted off the stage. It gave Jimmy a fresh realization of how he hated to see anyone hurt, and how imperfectly people lived in the world a perfect God gave to them.

Jimmy loved preaching, and took his material from anywhere he could find it. He got hold of tracts and preached from those; he preached sermons his father had prepared; he went to crusades and revivals to hear popular preachers of the day such as Lester Roloff and preached what he heard them preach. He preached at church camps, rest homes, Sunday school classes, and anywhere else he was invited.

In 1951 the family moved to Houston, where Brother Draper took the pulpit of Park Memorial Baptist Church, the third largest in the city. Jimmy spent the rest of the school year in Jacksonville, then followed the family to their new home, where he plunged into his own ministry, preaching at the Star of Hope shelter for men downtown, social events, and even at school.

Not long after Jimmy enrolled as a junior at Milby High School, he and some other students asked permission to form a Christian Student Union. The principal told them they had to get a thousand signatures on a petition before they could go forward.

Undeterred, Jimmy and his friends gathered the names, and Jimmy was elected as the first CSU president on campus. The organization sponsored devotionals twice a week in the school auditorium.

Jimmy headed his first official youth-led revival at Mason Drive Baptist Church in January 1953. Originally the event was scheduled for one week, but attendance was so high it was extended to two weeks—in part at the request of area high school principals. During that time there were over four hundred professions of faith. It was a promising start for the young preacher.

Jimmy teamed up with two other talented high school evangelists to conduct revivals anywhere within driving distance of Houston that they could get a booking. Jimmy shared preaching duties with his friend Charles Dan Oglesby, and Charles Swindoll led the music. (Jimmy could also sing if the need arose. Before Swindoll joined the team, Charles Dan and Jimmy took turns as song leader while the other preached.)

Perhaps the peak in this evangelistic team's history came in May 1953, when Billy Graham arrived for his first Houston Crusade, held at Rice Stadium on the Rice Institute campus. Jimmy's dad was a member of the executive committee for the Houston Crusade, and Charles Dan's father was head usher. The last night of the crusade, Roy Rogers and Dale Evans were appearing to share their testimonies. Two of the biggest cowboy stars in the movies, Roy and Dale also made records and were on the brink of another triumph as stars in the new entertainment world of television. Charles Dan and Jimmy finagled the job of escorting Roy and Dale to the speaker's platform from the ramp across the stadium field where the teams usually ran in.

The boys and their fathers arrived early, and Jimmy had the chance to meet Billy, Cliff Barrows, and George Beverly Shea before the service began. Then the boys stationed themselves at the ramp and, as part of the climax of the evening, Jimmy escorted Dale, and Charles Dan escorted Roy the length of the stadium to the roar of tens of thousands of people applauding. It was a triumphant night for the cause of Christ, and one Jimmy Draper would never forget.

A few days later, the stars and the roaring crowds were gone and Jimmy, Charles Dan Oglesby, and Charles Swindoll picked up their own revival ministry where they'd left off. There weren't always Hollywood personalities ready to share their testimonies with an admiring audience, but there were always people hungry for the saving message of salvation.

CHAPTER 5

ON THE ROAD

T HERE WAS NEVER ANY DOUBT in Jimmy Draper's mind where he would go to college. Growing up as Arkansas Baptists, his father and grandfather naturally went to Ouachita. As a Baptist in Texas, Jimmy's sights were naturally set from an early age on Baylor University, the most prestigious of all the Southern Baptist universities.

Baylor held its first classes in 1845 at Independence, in the Republic of Texas. Chartered by the Texas Baptist Educational Society, the school was named for the society's president, Robert Emmet Bledsoe Baylor, a lay preacher and associate justice of the Texas Supreme Court. Sam Houston, president of the Republic of Texas and himself a Baptist, gave the new school $330 and his law books.

As the village of Independence faded following the Civil War, nearby Waco boomed with the arrival of the railroads in 1881. In 1886 Baylor was moved to Waco, consolidated with Waco University (founded 1861), and issued a new charter under the control of the Baptist General Convention of Texas. There were other Baptist colleges in Texas, but none had the appeal or the reputation of Baylor, which had more students than all the rest combined.

When he lived in Jacksonville, Jimmy had driven with his family once in a while to Baylor for football games. In the fall of 1953 he enrolled there as a freshmen. His move to Waco from Houston broke up the Draper/Oglesby/Swindoll youth-led revival team at least temporarily, but they had had a good run, with more than twenty revivals held between January and September of that year.

Tackling his first-year curriculum didn't keep Jimmy from the pulpit for long. He was soon back on the revival circuit as much as his schedule would allow. Since revival preaching was scarcely profitable, he also got a job as a cafeteria busboy.

In the summers when there was no studying to do, Jimmy ramped up his revival schedule and pursued preaching at every opportunity around Houston and across East Texas. By the time he finished his second year at Baylor, the summer before his junior year was booked solid with preaching engagements except for a single week. Then he got a call asking him to come that week too. The song leader scheduled for a revival in Lake Jackson had gotten sick and cancelled at the last minute, and Jimmy was invited to take his place. Though he was a good and experienced music leader, Jimmy had been doing less of that lately in order to concentrate on preaching. But he had the open date, and the need was genuine. After giving it some thought, he accepted.

On the appointed date Jimmy joined the revival team in Lake Jackson and met with the pastor, who was new to the church. Among the information and advice he gave to the worship leaders, he told Jimmy he should get to know a popular senior in the high school youth group there named Carol Ann Floyd.

When they were introduced early in the revival, Jimmy was suddenly glad that he had accepted the last-minute work after all, and grateful to the pastor at Lake Jackson for his suggestion. Carol Ann was not only a dedicated member of the youth group and the choir, she was an attractive and popular girl. She had been elected Most Beautiful out of a student body of two thousand at Brazosport High School, and was a baton twirler and head majorette in the band. The two got along well from the start. Carol Ann accompanied Jimmy on visitations during the week, and even helped him wash the well-used car he'd named Herschel.

Carol Ann's mother saw her daughter becoming infatuated with the handsome, athletic young song leader. One night she warned her, "You know evangelists are a lot like sailors: they have a girl in every port!"

"Oh Mom!" Carol Ann exclaimed, "You know that's not true!" That Friday night as she sat in the choir loft, Carol Ann saw an unfamiliar girl come in and take a seat in the congregation. Sure enough, she had come from another revival of Jimmy's to hear him again. It was true that a lot of high school age boys and girls went in groups from one revival in the area to another, renewing friendships and enjoying their time together (Jimmy later tagged them "revival groupies"). But Jimmy didn't escort the strange girl home that night. He escorted Carol Ann. "Mother was part right," she decided afterward.

When Jimmy went back to Baylor, he and Carol Ann started writing to each other. It was a lively correspondence that both young people enjoyed. Jimmy wrote every day, and Carol Ann's mother left the letter for her on a round table in the front room. When she got home from school, Carol Ann made a beeline for the table, scooped up the letter, took it to her room, and read it three times or so. Then she put it away, knowing she'd get another one the next day. She wondered how much he spent every month on the rolls of three-cent stamps he must run through. It was clear from his letters how deeply he loved the Lord, and how sure he was that he would be a pastor one day.

Because she had surrendered her life for special service and fully expected to become "an old maid missionary schoolteacher in Africa," she knew she wasn't cut out to be a pastor's wife. Pastors stayed busy all the time; their families were constantly under a microscope; their wives had to entertain visitors and teach Bible school and play the piano and sing; their kids didn't get to be normal. These were the thoughts of a seventeen-year-old high school senior whose father had a "normal" eight-to-five job, but who felt herself falling in love.

She turned to the Lord in prayer: "Lord, You're going to have to help me because I'm falling in love with Jimmy Draper. You're going to have to take this love out of my heart because I'm not preacher's wife material."

She made a list of the attributes she thought a preacher's wife should have on one side of a sheet of paper, then started a list of her own abilities on the other. Try as she might, her second list was stalled at one entry: a twirler in the band. It wasn't a talent a church was likely to call on her for.

Then she sensed the Lord answering her prayer: "I haven't called you for what *you* can do, but for what *I* can do through you." Carol Ann took the Lord at His word by faith and fell in love, having no idea what the Lord had in store for her future.

She showed her mother the list of pastor's wife attributes and compared it with her one-entry list of accomplishments. "What about my twirling?" she asked.

With a smile her mother replied, "Use it or lose it."

"So," Carol Ann said later, "I buried it!"

The courtship continued by mail, with Jimmy and Carol Ann visiting occasionally during the weekends. Mr. and Mrs. Floyd were surprised at how fast the relationship developed. The Floyds had dated for seven years before they married and thought so quick a romance, especially a long distance one, could be unwise. Whether or not Jimmy knew at the time about Carol Ann's worry over the prospect of being a preacher's wife, he knew in his own heart that she was the girl he wanted to spend the rest of his life with. Over Thanksgiving he bought an engagement ring.

Christmas week, December 20, 1955, Jimmy and Carol Ann were engaged. They had known each other four months and had never lived in the same town during that time. But Carol Ann trusted her heart. She had come to know who Jimmy was by what he wrote. What she didn't know until years later was that her mother had come to know him in the same way. She secretly read every one of his letters too.

(Years later Carol Ann's mother told her the night before undergoing surgery that she had something to confess: She had read Jimmy's letters. "I watched you fall in love with a man I didn't know," she explained. "Mom," Carol Ann answered, "if I'd known you were interested I would have read them to you!")

Jimmy formally asked Mr. Floyd for his daughter's hand. Remembering his own long courtship and considering that his daughter was still in high school, Floyd agreed but with the request, "Son, I'd like you to wait as long as possible."

Thus the long distance romance became a long distance engagement. Carol Ann and her mother started making preparations for the wedding in Lake Jackson. Only a few weeks before the ceremony, Carol Ann's parents brought her to visit Jimmy in Waco. The engaged couple went to a friend's house to listen to records and after a while put on a Frank Sinatra song titled, "You Are My Everything." As they listened Carol Ann thought how true that was, not so much when it came to loving each other but of their loving Christ. The only way they could truly love each other was to love Jesus most of all and love each other through Him. With Sinatra singing on, they knelt together beside the couch and dedicated their lives and their marriage to Christ.

It turned out that "as long as possible" between engagement and marriage was only seven months, yet Carol Ann's father gave his full consent to the abbreviated courtship. Carol Ann graduated from high school in May, and she and Jimmy were married at First Baptist Church of Lake Jackson on July 14, 1956. The next week they were back in their Waco apartment, Jimmy was back in class as a senior at Baylor, Carol Ann was enrolled as a freshman, and they were both looking for jobs. He was also elected president of the Ministerial Alliance at Baylor for the year.

Three weeks after their marriage Jimmy began serving his first pastorate at Saints Rest Baptist Church in Bryan. Undergraduate though he was, he had solid preaching experience under his belt; in fact, his first Sunday at Saints Rest was almost six years to the day after he preached his first sermon in Mixon.

Jimmy took on his new duties at Saints Rest with enthusiasm. Preaching was nothing new to him, but establishing a household was something completely different. Other than their clothes, the only thing the newlyweds owned was their car. Lois Draper sent out an SOS at Park Memorial Church in Houston, and soon Jimmy and Carol Ann's modest apartment in Waco, and the parsonage in Bryan, were simply but fully furnished with donated furniture and accessories. Until the school year ended the young couple migrated back and forth each week, spending the school week in Waco and the weekend at the parsonage.

The Drapers always got to Bryan early enough in the weekend to spend all day Saturday visiting people in the neighborhood, sharing the gospel with them, and inviting them to church.

Jimmy's father had faithfully done that for years, considering it an essential part of his mission, and his mother had always gone with him in spite of her disability. Jimmy carried on this family pastoral tradition with Carol Ann by his side.

Jimmy graduated from Baylor in the spring of 1957 with straight As in his senior year, all the more impressive since he was not only a student but also a husband and pastor. By fall he added the role of father to the list when their son James Randall was born September 8, 1957.

In the same way there had never been any doubt in Jimmy's mind where he would go to college, there was no doubt where he would go to seminary. His father and grandfather both had graduated from Southwestern Baptist Theological Seminary in Fort Worth, and he had every intention of doing the same. He wondered, though, how and whether to leave his congregation at Saints Rest and how he and his growing family would get by without the job at Waldrup's. Placing his future in God's hands, he enrolled at Southwestern in January 1958, traveling to preach in Bryan now from Fort Worth on weekends, and giving up his Bryan employment to drive a bookmobile in Fort Worth.

Every year the Baptist Student Union Department took many requests for revival teams and sent its students out to fulfill them. Jimmy wanted to continue with his revival preaching, but he hesitated to do it unless there were enough engagements to justify leaving his young family alone week after week. He decided if he got ten engagements he'd go on the road for the summer. It was a decision modeled—consciously or not—after the biblical story of the fleece in Judges 6. Gideon asks for a sign from God that he will be victorious in battle and leaves a fleece of wool on the threshing floor. The next morning the fleece is wet with dew, but the surrounding ground is dry. This is the specific sign Gideon asked for.

Jimmy's "fleece of wool" was ten revivals during the summer, more than any other student had scheduled. He got twelve.

The next step was to ask the deacons at Steep Hollow for the time off to preach twelve revivals. Most of the deacons thought their young pastor should have the opportunity, but not all agreed. One believed if Jimmy wanted to maintain that kind of revival schedule he should resign as pastor. After a long, searching season of prayer, Jimmy and Carol Ann decided that God's will for them was to do revivals. Dedicated and diligent though he had been, Pastor Jimmy had not had a single baptism at the church in his brief time there, though new members had joined; revival preaching opened up fresh opportunities for proclaiming the gospel. Jimmy resigned on cordial terms, Carol Ann took little Randy with her to her parents' house for the season, and Jimmy spent the summer of 1958 preaching youth revivals across the state of Texas.

"We hate to lose such a gifted preacher," the congregation told Jimmy, "but we hate it even worse losing a good first baseman on the church softball team!" Then they teased, "You can go if you need to, but Carol Ann has to stay!"

In the fall of that year Jimmy became interim pastor of a small church in Talco, Texas. For nine months he and Carol Ann drove the 150 miles each way from Fort Worth and back every weekend. They traveled to Talco on Saturday, Jimmy preached Sunday morning and evening services, then they left Talco and got home around two a.m. If they had thirty-five cents to spare for the toll, they could save time taking the Dallas-Fort Worth Turnpike part of the way—an exceptional highway during those pre-Interstate years. Sometimes they had the money handy, sometimes they scrambled around and found it loose in drawers or under cushions before they got on the road, and sometimes they took the long way home.

When Jimmy took the interim pastorate in Talco, Carol Ann worked for an engineering company in Fort Worth. Hearing from her friends that the oil companies in town paid more, she gave two weeks' notice to her employer and lined up something better. It was then she found out she was expecting again. She had just resigned from a job paying a handsome $175 a month, and now that she was pregnant, she knew no one would hire her.

She and Jimmy prayed for guidance and for God to work His will through them. Within weeks Jimmy was offered his first full-time pastorate, in Iredell, Texas. It was a big and exciting step for the young family, and they could feel God's hand firmly guiding them. But it meant an even more brutal schedule than they'd had in the past. The Drapers moved to Iredell, and Jimmy essentially continued his seminary classes while holding down a new full-time job. And it was there on February 11, 1960, that their second child, Bailey Ray, was born.

The growing family settled into a grueling schedule. Four days a week Jimmy left the house at five in the morning and made the rounds to Walnut Springs, Morgan, Rio Vista, and Blum, where other seminary students lived who carpooled together. They drove a total of eighty-five miles to Fort Worth, then eighty-five miles back home that night. Carol Ann and the boys, with no second car, spent the day around the house. There were neighbors to visit with, and fortunately town was only a short walk away. And there were always diapers to wash.

Jimmy got home around six thirty every night. One winter day it was too cold to hang diapers out on the line, so Carol Ann strung them back and forth across a line in the kitchen. The first time it happened, Jimmy came home, started with surprise, then said with mock seriousness, "Excuse me, ma'am, I must be in the wrong house. There aren't any diapers in my kitchen!" He turned to leave. "Get in here, you!" his wife answered with a laugh, and the burdens of the day melted instantly away.

The letters that chronicled their romance had been bundled away for safekeeping, but about this time Jimmy decided to dispose of them a different way. His parents too had been faithful letter writers and had exchanged love letters every day for four years. No one else ever read them until the day Jimmy's brother George decided it would be fun to play mailman. He grabbed a packet of the secret letters, got on his bicycle, and put them in people's mailboxes up and down the street for two blocks in each direction. When Jimmy heard the story, he retrieved his and Carol Ann's letters and burned them. He couldn't run the risk of anyone else reading them. Besides, they'd served their purpose (though years later he called it "a big mistake").

The seminary years and the Iredell pastorate were lean times but good ones at the Draper house, filled as it was with hope and joy and contentment as only a godly home can be. The family never seemed to have anything extra, but they never did without the necessities. There was always enough money to put food on the table and gas in the tank. By the time Jimmy graduated from Southwestern in January 1961 a third little Draper was on the way. And around that same time God presented a new opportunity for the freshly minted divinity graduate and his family, in the form of a well-dressed group of strangers who unexpectedly came to call one snowy winter morning.

CHAPTER 6

A NEW SEASON

S NOW WAS AN UNCOMMON SIGHT in Iredell, Texas. An hour and a half drive south of Fort Worth, the town sat at the edge of the dry central Texas plain. Even so, there were still times when Canadian winter storms roared down over the Great Plains, across Oklahoma, and against the walls of the Iredell Baptist Church.

One bleak Sunday morning early in 1961, the congregation of Iredell Baptist and every other church in town awoke to bitter cold and surrounding fields and pastures covered with snow and ice. Because weather like this was so rare, people had to pay special attention to their livestock. The cold snap never lasted more than a day or two, then the ice would melt; until it did, many folks stayed close to home to keep an eye on their animals; they could ill afford to lose such an investment.

As people arrived at the church, stamping the slush from their feet on the porch before walking through the door, it was clear that only a few would brave the slick roads to attend worship. That made it all the more surprising to see a group of half a dozen or so strangers come in and take seats in the pew. To Carol Ann they "stuck out like a sore thumb." She knew without a doubt that it was a search committee looking for a new pastor.

A hallmark of the Baptist denomination is its lack of a central authority. The same priesthood of the believer that, while allowing complete freedom of conscience, makes it so hard to define Baptist beliefs precisely, also prescribes that each congregation have complete freedom to select and compensate its own pastor. There is no theological hierarchy like the Catholic College of Cardinals, and no administrative chain of command like the presbytery of the Presbyterians. Pastors are not appointed or assigned but called by each church acting independently. Pastors wanting to change churches get the word out through a grapevine of friends and colleagues; churches looking for a pastor accept recommendations, look at résumés, and appoint pulpit committees to recommend candidates. Usually the committee's work includes going to hear a prospective pastor in his current church.

The six strangers in dark suits liked what they saw and heard that bleak midwinter day. They wrote offering him the pulpit at Temple Baptist Church of Tyler, in the heart of East Texas not far from the Piney Woods camp where he had rededicated his life to serving Christ, though at the time he wasn't sure exactly what that meant. It was an unaccustomed feeling for Jimmy to be offered a new position and opportunity for service right out of the blue.

The timing was providential: Jimmy had just finished his seminary degree, and it was a good point to make a new start in his pastoral career. It wasn't that he was looking for a new church. He and Carol Ann were content to bloom where the Lord planted them and would have been willing to stay at Iredell indefinitely. Just finishing school and being able to concentrate full time on his church was exciting enough. Jimmy also enjoyed the local sports scene, announcing local football games and refereeing basketball. But God seemed to be calling him to a new place.

He and Carol Ann had been looking forward to settling down in Iredell now that his seminary studies were finished. There would be no more 170-mile daily round trips to classes. Jimmy could get to know his sons better: three-year-old Randy and Bailey, who had just turned one, had lived their whole lives with their daddy in school. Carol Ann too had anticipated having Jimmy home more, shoring up gains the church had made these past few months and getting more involved in the community. Nor would she mind a little help around the house: she was seven months pregnant with little Draper number three.

But after thinking and praying about it, the young couple decided the Lord was calling them to Tyler. Their congregation was sad to hear of the decision, but respected it because they knew it had been covered in prayer, and would mean new ministry opportunities for Brother Jimmy. His last week in Iredell he baptized thirteen teenagers. One young woman made her decision for Christ and wanted to be baptized on the spot even though she hadn't planned on it and didn't have a change of clothes. At her insistence, Jimmy baptized her in her black silk church dress. She also made him promise to come back in the summer and conduct her wedding. It was a promise Jimmy happily made, and faithfully kept. Draper graduated from Southwestern Seminary in January, and by March 1 had resigned his pastorate in Iredell to accept the call from Temple Baptist Church in Tyler, Texas.

Within a few weeks of the Drapers' arrival in Tyler, 150 miles or so to the east of Iredell, Jimmy and Carol Ann welcomed their third child, Terri Jean, into the family on April 13. The boys loved Tyler and their new house, and Carol Ann felt sure Terri would enjoy it just as much. Carol Ann was delighted with the new surroundings too. There was room in the yard to play, friendly neighbors, and enough storage space in their house that, after five years of marriage, she could finally retrieve the china she had stored at her mother's in Lake Jackson since her wedding.

This was the beginning of a new season in Jimmy's ministry. For the first time he was starting a pastorate without the distractions of school, a punishing commute, or a part-time second job. None of this had kept him from doing good work and earning the love and friendship of his congregation in the past. But now he could put all of his time and energy into leading his church. The potential seemed almost endless as Jimmy recalled the biblical metaphor of a mission field "white with harvest."

Brother Jimmy was a prolific correspondent and kept up a lively exchange of letters with several of his favorite professors from Southwestern. Virtus Gideon, professor of Old Testament, and Leon McBeth, professor of church history and an old carpool companion, were two he often wrote. He was always looking for good sermon outlines and advice on various aspects of his work, and these men were happy to give it. He regularly sought revivalists to come to Temple Baptist and accepted invitations himself to preach and lead revivals at other churches. There were also endless conferences and symposiums to attend or discuss.

In the summer of 1961 Temple Baptist had a weekly Sunday school attendance of about 180, twice the size of Brother Jimmy's first church at Steep Hollow. (Baptist churches traditionally take attendance in Sunday school, and those figures are generally used in discussing average attendance, being more accurate than estimates of the number attending worship. Membership rolls are notoriously inaccurate gauges of the functional size of a church body.) Continuing the tradition he had so enthusiastically embraced during his high school days, he organized a youth-led Crusade for Christ in July, with preaching from a seventeen-year-old visiting revivalist named Richard Cheatham. The sight of it must have brought back memories of those exciting summers in Houston with Chuck Swindoll and Charles Dan Oglesby. Besides, that was not so long ago; the past eight years sometimes seemed like a blur.

The church also hosted a youth retreat that summer, and the regular teen-time for high schoolers every week had blossomed under Jimmy's leadership, averaging forty-three per week from fourteen the year before. The young pastor had waited on the Lord and gone where he thought He was leading, and the Lord was richly blessing his ministry.

Like all his previous churches, Temple Baptist was predominately working class. The members there were not hungry for the rarefied theological arguments that might most readily appeal to a recent seminary graduate. What they wanted was a clearer understanding of the Bible and how it could help them get through the week. Jimmy was a keen and enthusiastic student of theology, yet he knew how to bring all the high-flying theories down to earth. He preached from the Bible, not from the headlines, but he made it clear how the two are connected: the Bible contains everything people need to know about how to make decisions and live their lives in the modern world. Christianity was not complicated. It was something the simplest person or the youngest child could understand.

A revealing example of Brother Jimmy's approach to teaching the bedrock truths of Christianity came in a letter to one Mr. Charles Bryan Stephenson of Tyler when he was only a few days old:

Dear Chuck:

My, what a joy it is to welcome you into this world
of ours! We are so proud of you and thank the Lord
Jesus for sending you our way. I want to commend you
upon your choice of parents. You could have looked
the world over and not have made a better choice!
Your mother and daddy are wonderful people and will
lead you to love them very much.

This is a wonderful world that you have come into.
There are so many beautiful things for you to see and
to learn about. You will hear mommie and daddy tell
you about the trees, rivers, grass, animals, stars, sun,
moon, people, mountains, ocean, fish, birds, and a
thousand other things. You will love all of them. Best of
all you will hear mommie and daddy tell you about
Baby Jesus and how He grew into a man and died that
we might be saved. I know you will want to know Him
as personal Savior when you reach the age of understanding and will give your precious heart to Him. And
as you do that wonderful thing you will want to let
Him use your life each day. All of these things are
before you and I want you to love every moment of life
that God gives to you!

The world is a beautiful place, but I fear that we
have not left it a very good world for you to come into.
We have wasted many opportunities to make it a better
world and we must pass it on to you with the sincere
prayer that you will succeed far better than we have
done in making this world a better world. We trust that
you will do just that!

God bless you Chuck, and may you find abiding joy
and happiness every day that you live is my sincere
prayer, in Jesus' name.

Word spread quickly about the dynamic new preacher in Tyler.
His sermons were thought-provoking but easy to understand; his
Wednesday and Sunday night programs were setting new attendance records; his guest revivalists were varied and inspiring. It
wasn't long before other pulpit committees were probing for signs
he might be willing to move again.

Jimmy had not been looking to move when he accepted the
pulpit in Tyler, and he wasn't looking to move now. As various
inquiries kept coming in, Jimmy went ahead with planning for
conferences, revivals, and other special events into the next year.
In the fall, Jimmy got letters from four churches in three weeks
asking about his interest in moving, including one from his friend
Bill Tomerlin, director of the Baptist Student Union of San
Antonio.

Tomerlin had been invited to serve as interim pastor of
University Park Baptist Church in San Antonio beginning in
January 1962. The elderly pastor there had been in poor health for
the last two years or so, and the church had "steadily declined"
during that time. "This church has a good future," Tomerlin
wrote.

It is located in a relatively strong neighborhood. The
constituency is a strong middle class, good, hard working people, with enough trained people to have a
strong organization. . . . It needs a good, zealous, evangelistic preacher . . . .

Jimmy I know that you have not been at Temple
very long, and you may not be interested at all in moving. But ever since I have known that [Pastor Hal]

Wingo was leaving I have thought of you and that
church.

Tomerlin was right in guessing Draper was in no hurry to
move. In his reply, Jimmy outlined his position, which was the
same one he would take through the years when considering
future moves:

> I am not interested in moving at this time, but I do
> not believe that I will ever really feel that I am. God
> will impress it upon me when the time to move comes
> and He will need the help of someone to get me before
> other churches. If you feel that you should recommend
> me to the church, go ahead. Like I said, we are very
> happy here . . . and do not have any desire to change
> right now. However, if God leads, that is another mat-
> ter. . . . So, as you feel led, you act and we will let the
> Lord take care of the rest of it.

Furthermore, Jimmy had been wondering, now that his seminary studies were completed, whether he should continue as a
pastor or whether he should serve the kingdom in some other
way. He loved preaching revivals and had done that twice as long
as he had been a pastor. As his friend and former professor Leon
McBeth had recently done, he could get his doctorate.

In a letter to McBeth on December 4, 1961, amidst talk of winter colds and smallpox vaccinations for the children, Draper
shared some of the uncertainty he felt about his future:

> The work here is going well, but so much needs to
> be done. Pray for us. I still do not feel completely
> happy in the pastorate, so don't know what the Lord is
> going to do with me. I think I must be his problem
> child.

Two days later, Professor McBeth sent a heartfelt response:

> Jim, how true it is that the Lord calls men to other
> ministries than the pastorate as my own work testifies
> in my own conviction. Yet these last two years more
> and more convince me that today's crucial and deter-
> minative ministry is not denominational, classroom,
> itineration, but pastoral. The PASTORS can help
> Southern Baptists recover their spiritual equilibrium—
> nobody else. No place of service, in my view, is more
> on God's firing line than the pulpit of a N. T. church.

Jimmy continued preaching, and the church in Tyler continued to strengthen and grow to the point where it was running out of room. After only a few months in the pulpit Jimmy led a drive to remodel the church sanctuary. The renovations were a great success in every way but one. The acoustics had been modified so dramatically that the congregation experienced the unfamiliar sensation of hearing themselves sing. The shock of their own voices stunned them into a quiet murmur, and it was a while before they were confident enough to get back to singing full voice.

Brother Draper had not pursued the lead on the church in San Antonio, and the pastor there retired in January as planned. Within weeks a pulpit committee from University Park appeared at the newly decorated Temple Baptist Church. After the service they paid their respects to Jimmy and Carol Ann, then made the three-hundred-mile trip back home.

The offer wasn't long in coming. On January 31, the church secretary at University Park wrote Draper a letter to say that the pulpit committee there prayed he would "find peace of mind and a calmness of spirit from doing what God has planned for you."

She continued:

"From the first, we had hoped that we would have a unanimous feeling that when we found the right man we would definitely know it. We each felt that way in your service Sunday, we were sure that you were that man. Your forceful delivery, your ease in the pulpit, your Bible teachings were all that we had been looking for."

Two weeks later Jimmy, accompanied by his wife, was in San Antonio "preaching in view of a call," essentially an audition sermon of a pastor before a Baptist congregation whose pulpit committee has decided to recommend him. After the sermon—from a day to a week or two later—the congregation votes whether or not to call the visiting preacher as its new pastor.

Still Jimmy resisted the idea of a move, writing to a friend and fellow pastor, "We do not feel inclined to accept the church, but their committee is so unanimous and has expressed such strong feelings that we cannot find peace on the matter without going [to preach in view of a call]. I really do not want to leave Tyler just yet and especially for San Antonio, but we will let the Lord lead. Pray for us this weekend."

University Park was twice the size of Temple, with the immediate prospect of further significant growth. The field was white with harvest, but for the last several years the church had not been able to act on the opportunities before them. The previous pastor's illness had kept the church from reaching its potential, and the leadership was eager to get beyond the current plateau and on to new heights of service.

Did the Lord want the Drapers in San Antonio?

It was a much bigger city than Tyler, but with a small-town feel because of the way the population was divided by history and heritage into groups that tended not to intermix: a large Hispanic population, a legacy of San Antonio's days as a Spanish colonial capital; one of the country's largest concentrations of retired military veterans, thanks to the huge army and air force training installations around the city; and the rest of the residents, many of them descendants of the early American settlers that moved west and settled the region in the 1830s.

As great as the challenges at University Park were, the opportunities were even greater. It would be hard to leave the good friends and wonderful opportunities of Tyler behind. Jimmy had a newly remodeled sanctuary and a booming ministry. That was a church worth holding on to. It was also a church that was healthy and on a strong upward trend. Perhaps God was telling the Drapers that their work in Tyler was finished, and a new work elsewhere was prepared.

Jimmy and Carol Ann talked to each other and to God about it faithfully and fervently. Praying together about big decisions was an integral part of their relationship, and the process would become even more familiar in years to come as other offers and opportunities arose. San Antonio needed an answer soon; after a time of sincere prayer that answer came. Almost a year to the day after beginning his ministry at Temple Baptist, Jimmy and his family said good-bye to their friends in Tyler and headed for the Alamo City.

CHAPTER 7

PASTORAL LIFE

BROTHER JIMMY KNEW UNIVERSITY PARK was a church in decline. He had scarcely moved into his new office before he began digging deeper into the history of the church, taking stock of the challenges he faced and how to meet them. At the root of the situation was the fact that the previous pastor had stayed in the pulpit beyond his time. His long illness had led to inactivity that affected everything. There was a feeling of listlessness and stagnation in the youth program, adult ministries, community outreach, evangelism, and every other aspect of church. Responsibility had not been delegated, so that when the pastor wasn't on hand to make the decisions, encourage the membership, and shepherd a project forward, the momentum for it died off. It was like a powerful but rudderless ship, ready to go anywhere but without anyone to do the steering.

Underperforming though it was, University Park was still twice the size of Temple Baptist. Before he could build the ministry of the congregation, he had to solidify what was there. Within weeks there was a new feeling of excitement not only in the church but also in the surrounding community. Brother Jimmy and his family brought a faster pace and a new sense of opportunity to the people there, and they responded with enthusiasm.

Carol Ann loved her new home. San Antonio was her birthplace, though she had lived there only a short while before moving on to Houston and Lake Jackson. It was a friendly, welcoming city, and after the first week, Carol Ann felt like she'd lived there all her life. Randy would start school the next fall, with Bailey following him a year later.

San Antonio was the biggest city Jimmy had worked in as a full-time pastor, and he relished getting to know the other Baptist pastors in town. One characteristic of his ministry that made him successful was his love of relationships. He cultivated a wide circle of friends, kept up with colleagues from seminary days and his previous pastorates, and immersed himself in the lives and needs of his congregation.

He was a tireless note writer, answering every letter to him promptly and sending a steady stream of thank-yous and congratulations. When he went to preach a revival and stayed in someone's home, they received a note of thanks for their hospitality within a day or two. Church members, their children and friends, public officials, newspaper editors—all could depend on a letter from Pastor Jimmy whenever congratulations, encouragement, or correction were in order.

The range of his correspondence reflected his range of interest in community affairs. If he was moved by a news report on television, the station manager got a note of encouragement. When he was especially impressed with a new kind of razor blade, he wrote to tell the manufacturer so. When a car dealer Jimmy traded with asked him to corroborate the fact that there were 47,000 miles on his trade-in when there were actually 87,000, he let the dealer know exactly what he thought about the proposal.

Jimmy was a pastor and leader who never considered himself above his audience. To him a preacher wasn't some remote authority figure but a man who fully involved himself in the life of the church. When the deacons challenged the boys to a game of basketball he gladly agreed to join the deacons' team; when they decided their uniform would be T-shirts and pink leotards, he suited up with everybody else—to the delight of the crowd.

Before the end of 1962 it was clear that University Park Baptist Church had reversed course; it was solid and growing stronger every week. It was also running out of room. Jimmy saw what excitement had been generated back in Tyler when the church there was renovated. The church in San Antonio, he believed, was ready for an even more ambitious project: a new building. The Lord had not only stopped the decline but was improving attendance to the point where space was tight. The challenge was no longer coming up with program ideas and getting people to execute them, but scheduling activities so that there was room enough for everybody who wanted to take part.

There wasn't enough money in the church to build a building debt-free, and Jimmy didn't want to borrow money from a bank, so of the building budget of $175,000 the church issued $140,000 worth of construction bonds, encouraging members to buy them. The church essentially borrowed money from itself, using the cash to pay for construction, then paying back the bond value plus interest over several years. Church financial advisors recommended this as a way to finance expansion projects internally, and often bought some of the bonds themselves.

During the year of bond promotion, design, and construction, Jimmy kept a close eye on the fiscal health of the church while pursuing a full agenda of special programs, revivals, and his own preaching and evangelistic work out of town. One winter weekend he and Carol Ann went to Dallas for a state evangelism conference and spent some time with a friend from seminary days named George Harris, then pastor of East Henderson Baptist Church, Cleburne, Texas. George and his wife hadn't planned to spend the night, but a terrible blizzard came up and they couldn't drive home. All hotel rooms in the area were soon snapped up, leaving the Harrises stranded. Jimmy and Carol offered to let them share their room.

The next morning, Jimmy's father (who had moved to Marshall, Texas, to accept a position as district missions secretary of the Baptist General Convention of Texas), also attending the conference, knocked on Jimmy's hotel room door. When he saw another couple in the room with Jimmy and Carol Ann, his eyes widened. "Son, you can't do that!" he exclaimed. The room burst into laughter. After he caught his breath, Jimmy explained what was going on. Jimmy later acknowledged his naïveté, but the story was good for a laugh for years to come.

After the pulpit committee from University Park had heard Brother Jimmy preach in Tyler, the first letter he got was from the church secretary in San Antonio, Martha Aaron. In the two years prior to Jimmy's arrival she had gradually taken on more oversight of office management, bookkeeping, and other chores. After the new pastor came, she was invaluable to him for her understanding of the way the church operated.

She had a favor to ask Brother Jimmy, but it took some time before she could gather up the courage to do it. It concerned her brother, Billy Aylward. He was an inmate at the state penitentiary in Lansing, Kansas, who was now a prisoner trusty and had a parole hearing coming up. Martha asked Jimmy to do whatever he could to improve her brother's chances of parole. Brother Jimmy and Billy started writing back and forth. Jimmy felt over time that he got to know Billy's heart and that Billy deserved a chance to prove himself on the outside. Jimmy also wrote the prison warden on Billy's behalf.

Billy was lonely, anxious, and frustrated that no one seemed to understand his side of the story. The warden was noncommittal, detached, and not inclined to sympathy. Jimmy wrote faithfully to Billy, encouraging him in every way he could think of and never giving up on the warden, even after repeated cold and unencouraging replies.

It was Jimmy who had the sad duty of writing to tell Billy his father had died. Though the pastor and the convict had never met, Brother Jimmy infused his message with warmth and hope as though he had known Billy for years: "I'm sorry that I could not be there to share this news with you in person but want to assure you that everything is all right here. . . . I believe that God spared your father for this extra week to ten days in order that you might have opportunity to write the very touching letters to him . . . and in order that he might assure all of us that he was more than ready to go. He gave a marvelous Christian testimony to everyone in the hospital. His doctor and I went to high school together over in East Texas, and he spoke of the tremendous Christian influence that your Dad had had."

Jimmy was never able to secure Billy's release, but his correspondence with Billy and the prison authorities led to freedom for one of Billy's friends. Dean Foster, another inmate at Lansing, qualified for parole if he could line up a job and a place to live. Jimmy found him a job with a church member and, with Carol Ann's agreement, told him he could live for the time being in the Drapers' garage apartment.

Foster was released, and came to San Antonio on the bus. The Drapers invited him to dinner, then showed him to his apartment.

If any of the family had concerns about housing an ex-con, no one mentioned it. In that part of San Antonio in the 1960s, nobody locked any doors at night. The Draper house was unairconditioned, which in central Texas meant the windows were open eight or nine months of the year. Because there was no sense of fear from the parents, the three children had no inkling they should worry about a thing. They thought having a visitor out back was fun.

The fun didn't last long. Dean started his job, worked hard, and went to church. He was in a low-paying job, habitually nervous, and had trouble adjusting to life as a free man; still Jimmy encouraged him, and wrote Billy about his progress. But one Sunday morning Dean had a visitor. Jimmy had already left for church and Carol Ann was getting the children dressed when a big gold Cadillac pulled into the driveway. Three men in suits got out and walked to the garage apartment. A short while later the three men and Dean got in the big car and drove away. It wasn't long afterward that Dean Foster disappeared for good. Word on the grapevine was that he had been lured back into the drug trade, which had gotten him imprisoned in the first place. But no one ever knew for sure.

In the summer of 1963 the new building at University Park was dedicated, and Jimmy invited church members, visitors, neighbors, and bond holders to a special celebration of thanksgiving. As he reported to a colleague, "Everything is going well here and we continue to be well pleased with the opportunity that God has given to us. Attendance is running high and God is blessing us in our efforts."

This was a time when Jimmy Draper could take a breather if he liked. His family was healthy, his church was prospering, and his parents and brothers were well. His father had returned to the pulpit after seven years in denominational service in Texas, accepting the pastorate of the First Baptist Church in Warren, Arkansas.

But relaxing wasn't Brother Jimmy's style. Where he knew there was a need he got involved even if it didn't directly affect him or his congregation. One example among many was a pilot program pairing healthy Southern Baptist churches in San Antonio with struggling Hispanic ones. The church that University Park was helping had its pastor leave for the mission field, fell deeply into debt to build a building in a more suitable neighborhood, and couldn't pay its monthly bills. The core of remaining members thought the church was a lost cause and hesitated to commit any more time or money. Brother Jimmy went to bat for them with the Baptist General Convention of Texas in Dallas:

> "The people have been gracious and cordial to me
> . . . . [The new pastor there] and I both feel that the
> problem right now is that the debt of the church build-
> ing is so tremendous on their shoulders that they have
> no incentive to work or do anything about the progress
> of the church. . . . If we can [forgive] the debt or sus-
> pend the payments for a year or two, perhaps this is
> the answer. . . . The location of the church is strategic.
> A community of nearly 10,000 people with no evangel-
> ical witness save this church stands to be the loser."

There were financial needs in the extended Draper family too, and Jimmy served as a sounding board for his father on the subject of his middle brother, George, who had bought some furniture he couldn't pay for, then moved it out of town.

"I have made an occasional payment," the elder
Draper wrote his son, "but have simply not been able

to keep it current. The latest threat is to have him arrested for moving mortgaged goods across the state line. I have sent them a post-dated check for one month's payment. I hope it will hold them off. The payments are only $15.71 a month, but I am simply unable to care for it as it needs to be. . . . I do not mean to burden you with my problems, but simply had to unload on someone, and I can't talk to anyone here about it, of course."

George was moving to San Antonio, but, the senior James emphasized, "I certainly do not want him to be a burden to you. Anything you can do to help him will be appreciated, but, after all, you didn't take him to raise. . . . Get him in church if you can; he hasn't been going lately, and it's my judgment that the Lord will never bless him, in school or otherwise, as long as he lays out like that. . . . [On the other hand, your brother] Charlie is doing extremely well, in school, church, etc. He will begin leading the music in our mission Wed. night."

Jimmy inherited his father's desire to see people support themselves whenever possible–even beloved family members–and he challenged able-bodied men and women to take responsibility for their own lives. His convictions sometimes drew sharp responses from his blue-collar congregation. After hearing Brother Jimmy preach, as the apostle Paul said, that those who would not work should not eat, an elderly woman sent a sharply worded letter and several clippings on illiteracy, bread lines, and other indicators of economic distress, insisting it was the Christian's job to care for the poor and unfortunate.

In a friendly yet thorough three-page reply, Jimmy emphasized the difference between people who were unable to work, whom

Christians were duty bound to help, and people who chose not to work, whom no one had an obligation to help:

> I have never refused to help any man who ever
> stopped by this office since I have been your pastor.
> I have bought meals with my own money, bought
> gasoline, provided groceries and clothing. The interest-
> ing thing is that many of those who come by ask for
> work, but really want you to give them something.
> Several have asked for work and when I put them to
> work and then pay them, they did not come back
> again. I do not feel it is ever wise to rob a man of his
> self-respect. When you pay a man not to work and care
> for him when he refuses to work you rob him of his
> pride and his self-respect. That is why I do not believe
> that governmental welfare for those who refuse to
> work should be available. . . . You and I as Christian
> people have a great responsibility to provide for those
> around us who cannot provide for themselves. But
> I believe the place of government is to make it possible
> for every man to provide for himself.

As he matured in his calling, Brother Jimmy felt his views on public policy issues becoming more confident, though he never used the pulpit as a political forum. Clearly a person's view of the world and world events was shaped by his spiritual convictions–or lack of them. He also developed strong views about a simmering theological divide that boiled over across the denomination during his years in San Antonio, with repercussions that would affect the rest of his career.

An early indication of his thinking comes in a letter to him dated July 9, 1963, from his long-time friend and frequent correspondent, Southwestern professor Leon McBeth:

Jimmy, I have gathered from your correspondence
that you are growing more conservative. Fine. Just
don't lose your sweet Christian spirit—as so many have.
Keep *perspective,* and respect those who may not be
quite so conservative as you are, and yet hold to the
basic Biblical faith also. Boy, all of a sudden I'm preaching to you! But I think you know what I mean, and if
I remember you, you will remain a Christian in spirit
and attitude at all times.

Behind this friendly admonition was an issue that had exposed
a deep divide among Southern Baptists. In some quarters, opponents in the matter couldn't even agree on what the question was,
much less how to resolve it. One thing that seemed clear was that
many seminary professors were calling for restraint and
perspective, while some pastors and laymen were calling into
question seminarians' adherence to foundational essentials of
Baptist theology.

The divergence of viewpoint came to light after the publication
of a Bible textbook two years before, igniting a controversy that
refused to fade away but got hotter instead. The disagreement
revolved around an issue that was almost as old as the denomination itself: Southern Baptists reject any written creed. While
that leaves members free to believe and act according to their
God-given conscience, it makes it impossible to define precisely
what qualifies as Baptist belief and what does not. Does a Baptist
have to believe that Genesis is literally true? Like some of their
brethren generations later, Baptist pastors and leaders in the
1960s tried to avoid taking a definitive stand on the question at
hand, which served only to make matters worse.

When it comes to truth and the Bible, there is no middle
ground.

CHAPTER 8

THE GENESIS OF DISCORD

T HE GREAT DIVIDE that began welling up among Southern Baptists in the early 1960s had historical precedent: the denomination's very beginning was rooted in a nationwide division that had been simmering since colonial days. America in the 1840s was a nation still divided over the propriety of slavery, with Baptists represented on both sides of the issue. The American Baptist Home Missions Society resolved not to support either slave owners or abolitionists, but then declined to act on an application by a slaveholder to be a missionary. Some slaveholding Baptists took this to mean the Society was interested in their money but not in their ministry.

On May 8, 1845, a group of them met in Augusta, Georgia, and formed the Southern Baptist Convention "for the purpose of eliciting, combining, and directing the energies of the Baptist denomination of Christians for the propagation of the gospel." As pastor and church historian Jerry Sutton later observed, this statement of purpose "was used to argue that the basis of unity was programmatic rather than theological." In other words, to some people a Southern Baptist from the beginning was defined by how he shared the gospel, not by what he thought the gospel meant.

This led to an element of confusion between conforming to an unspecified but generally held norm on one hand, and acknowledging individual freedom on the other, that Southern Baptists were never able to resolve. Historic Baptist theology was used to support widely differing viewpoints. Some denominational leaders insisted this was as it should be and that official Southern Baptist doctrine should never be so specific that it "excluded one tradition or another," as Sutton wrote, "thereby destroying denominational unity and undermining the missionary imperative."

From the beginning, some Southern Baptists felt alarmed by leaders who strayed from theological orthodoxy. James Petigru Boyce was the first president of Southern Baptist Theological Seminary. In his inaugural address, delivered at Furman University in 1856, Boyce warned that a single theological renegade could be a dangerous threat:

> The history of our own denomination in this country furnishes an illustration. Playing upon the prejudices of the weak and ignorant among our people, decrying creeds as an infringement upon the rights of conscience, making a deep impression by his extensive learning and great abilities, Alexander Campbell threatened at one time the total destruction of our faith. Had he occupied a chair in one of our Theological institutions, that destruction might have been completed. There would have been time to disseminate widely, and fix deeply, his principles, before it became necessary to avow them publicly; and when this necessity

arrived, it would have been attended by the support of
the vast majority of our best educated Ministers. Who
can estimate the evil which would have then ensued!

Campbell had sailed to America from his native Ireland in
1809 and formed a Baptist church with his father in Pennsylvania
in 1811. Many of his ideas were in harmony with Baptist beliefs—
no formal creed, authority of the Bible, baptism by immersion—
but there were differences that put him increasingly at odds with
the denomination. Finally in 1830, he separated from the Baptists
and formed a denomination of his own, the Disciples of Christ.

Boyce insisted that professors at Southern Seminary sign a
doctrinal statement called the Abstract of Principles, which one
group of Baptists derisively called a creed, lifting up the often-
heard refrain that Baptists have no creed but the Bible. Boyce
replied that the Abstract was "a safeguard as to the future teachings of the professors around the endowments which have been
raised for it."

There were Southern Baptists, Boyce later recalled, who would
rather "have abandoned our object, rather than aid in raising an
institution whose funds and endowment were not secured to the
maintenance of the principles and practices then prevalent, and
still prevailing in our Southern Zion." But, he added, "it was
equally important that upon these questions upon which there
was still a difference of opinion among Southern Baptists, the
Seminary articles should not bind the institution . . . . It is hoped
that the time will come when all Baptists shall see eye to eye upon
all points. But this is to be accomplished by mutual forbearance
and instruction."

The unanswered questions cycled through the history of
Southern Baptists again and again down through the years. First,
what exact theological belief made someone a Southern Baptist?

Second, what exact belief categorically excluded one from being Southern Baptist? Third, was the denomination founded in the first place over missionary outreach or doctrine?

As president emeritus of Southwestern Baptist Theological Seminary in 1986, Robert N. Naylor wrote, "Our problem [over adopting a statement of principles] is not a difference about the Scriptures, our problems are political." But the political problems seemed invariably to be caused by a lack of agreement over what Baptists ought to believe. Even a generation earlier a motion was made during the annual Convention meeting to appoint a committee "to investigate the charge that modernism now exists in the Southern Baptist Theological Seminary in Louisville, Kentucky."

James Boyce saw great potential danger in having theological liberals as seminary professors, and his premonition of the crisis that might result came eerily to life in 1961, the year Jimmy graduated from Southwestern and moved his family to Tyler.

That was the year Broadman Press, a publishing arm of the Baptist Sunday School Board, published *The Message of Genesis* by Dr. Ralph Elliott, a professor at Midwestern Baptist Theological Seminary in Kansas City, one of six seminaries supported by the denomination. The book was used as a seminary text despite Dr. Elliott's affirmation that much of Old Testament scripture was "parabolic and symbolic." He believed for example that Old Testament characters were not as old as the Scriptures claimed. "In all probability," Elliott wrote, "the Priestly writer simply exaggerated the ages in order to show the glory of an ancient civilization."

This viewpoint flew directly in the face of "The Baptist Faith and Message." This was a denominational statement issued in 1925 (despite the objection in some quarters that it too amounted to a "creed") that proclaimed the Bible was "truth without any mixture of error," which in turn came directly from the New Hampshire Confession of 1833. The statement, in some ways a historic echo of Boyce's "Abstract of Principles," was made in response to what Baptist leaders termed a "pervasive antisupernaturalism in the culture."

"The Baptist Faith and Message" explained that its words were "not intended to add anything to the simple conditions of salvation revealed in the New Testament," and should themselves not be considered "as complete statements of our faith, having any quality of finality or infallibility." It purported to be a defining statement of Baptist belief but not a definitive one: descriptive but not prescriptive.

Dr. Elliott was immediately criticized by Baptists who saw his views as incompatible with Southern Baptist teaching in general and "The Baptist Faith and Message" in particular. At the same time, Elliott's defenders rushed to insist that his views were within the framework of Southern Baptist thought, and that cultivating a diversity of viewpoints was essential to the education process and a desired result of academic freedom.

In January 1962 the trustees of Midwestern Seminary gave Dr. Elliott a vote of confidence, resolving, "we do affirm our confidence in him as a consecrated Christian, a promising scholar and teacher, a loyal servant of Southern Baptists, and a dedicated and warm evangelic preacher of the Gospel." But at the Southern Baptist Convention that summer in San Francisco, convention messengers sensed a rising tide of liberalism encroaching upon traditional doctrine in the pages of Elliott's book. In hopes of clarifying their position for the record, the Convention passed a resolution stating that the Bible was the "infallible Work of God," a position fully in keeping with "The Baptist Faith and Message" statement of 1925.

The Convention went on to recommend to the leadership of seminaries and other denominational entities that they "take such steps as shall be necessary to remedy at once those situations where such views now threaten our historic position." In other words, Elliott and his ilk had to go.

The Baptist Sunday School Board, which controlled Broadman Press, came down not surprisingly in Elliott's corner: "The elected Sunday School Board further encourages Broadman Press to continue to publish books which will represent more than one point of view and which will undergird faith and contribute to the Christian growth and development of those who read them."

The Baptist state newspaper in Kentucky weighed in on Elliott's side as well: "Elliott does not deserve a medal for extreme views compared with his fellow Southern Baptists. If he deserves a medal, it is for his courage in writing a book in which he honestly expresses his views. Some teachers who would share his approach to the Bible, though not necessarily his conclusions, feel his only mistake was to write down his conclusions at this time."

By the fall of 1962, the trustees of Midwestern Seminary had changed their stance and voted twenty-two to seven to dismiss Elliott. Even then, however, they squandered the opportunity to address head-on the core question that had been nagging at Southern Baptists since 1845: what exactly does a Baptist believe? Instead of stating Elliott's doctrinal position and specifically how it differed from what the trustees found acceptable, they fired him officially because he refused to agree not to republish *The Message of Genesis.*

Along with other Southern Baptist pastors in the early 1960s, Jimmy Draper had to look inside himself to see what he believed, then shepherd his congregation according to the truth God placed in his heart. The majority of pastors were surprised and appalled to see seminary professors defend viewpoints that directly challenged the concept of scriptural infallibility. Professors and seminary leaders were equally disturbed that the pursuit of knowledge and the preservation of academic freedom were, as they saw it, threatened by a narrow-minded and legalistic interpretation of "infallibility."

His friend Leon McBeth had remarked about Jimmy becoming "more conservative." But it wasn't that Jimmy was shifting his theological moorings; they were unchanged and unchangeable, easily recognizable to his father (and grandfather, had he been alive). It was that, like so many Southern Baptists, Jimmy had assumed everybody in the denomination believed the Bible was the true, complete, and infallible word of God, and held fast to that conviction even as the argument and shifting opinions swirled around the theological ground he stood on.

That's what he believed and that's what he preached. University Park Baptist Church embraced Brother Jimmy's teaching and his dedication, its Sunday school enrollment up 21 percent in three years to 730 and the annual budget expanding from $42,000 to $62,000, an increase of 47 percent. Remarkable as they were, numbers weren't what Brother Jimmy considered indicators of success. He explained exactly what he thought was important in responding to a church in Albuquerque that wrote looking for a new pastor and wondering if he would be interested in the position. An information form they sent him to fill out about his church and himself focused completely on budgets and enrollment:

I am somewhat disturbed that the questions asked
dealt only with the statistics of our church. None dealt
with my doctrinal convictions, etc., which are much
more vital. I have had a growing conviction that we are

much more concerned about statistics than we are people. Statistics in no way indicate the spiritual growth of a people and the quality of work being done. Some churches have greater opportunities than others for statistical growth, so this is an inaccurate and unfair gauge.

Leading revivals in Detroit, Chicago, Cincinnati, and New York during this period, Jimmy began to raise his profile outside Texas and Arkansas. Before he was thirty he had conducted ninety revivals in seven states. This strengthened the network of contacts that led to still other speaking and preaching opportunities. The deacons at University Park voted to allow him not only to continue guest preaching elsewhere, but to commute to graduate school as well, and he was accepted into a doctoral program. Honored as he was at the offer, he felt at the time that it might penalize the church, and that as busy as he was with his pastoral duties he couldn't "do it justice right now."

In the spring of 1965, in response to another request for information about him from a pastor search committee–this one in Madison, Wisconsin–Brother Jimmy articulated his doctoral position. It was as clear a statement as he ever gave on the subject, one that turned characteristically not on theological fine points but on bedrock Baptist beliefs:

    1. God–I believe that God is the eternal Creator and sustainer of the universe. He indwells the hearts of His children in the presence of the Holy Spirit. He longs to lead us to deeper understanding of His will and purpose for our lives.

    2. Christ–I believe that Jesus Christ was virgin-born. He is the eternal Son of God who is the perfect revelation of God. He is the Lord of our world and of His

children. The essence of the Christian life is the living of Christ in and through us.

3. Plan of Salvation–Man is saved as he confesses his need and his sin to God. He is saved through faith in Christ by the grace of God. Salvation is a gift of God to all who will receive it. Salvation involves a personal commitment to a personal God.

4. Bible–I believe the Bible to be the inspired Word of God. It is an accurate and infallible record of the revelation of God to man. It is our final authority in matters of faith and practice.

5. Baptism–The total immersion of a believer in Jesus Christ by a properly authorized person of a New Testament Church.

6. Lord's Supper–Symbol of the death of Christ, given to the church to remind us of that death and renew our commitment to Christ as we partake in it.

7. Church–Body of baptized believers united in a common faith for the purpose of carrying out the Kingdom of God in this world.

8. Christian's responsibility to others–The Christian has the glorious privilege and grave responsibility of sharing the gospel of our Lord to every person in this world of all nations, races, and classes. Every Christian is to be a preacher of the gospel of Christ. This is our only hope to capture a world for our Lord!

9. Stewardship of life and possessions–One-tenth of all that a man earns belongs to God. The nine-tenths is to be used under the direction and guidance of God. Every talent and ability that a man possesses is his responsibility to use for the glory of God.

These beliefs informed the way Brother Jimmy led his church and developed its programs. As pastor of five churches in less than ten years, he knew from experience what worked and what didn't. In letters he wrote and activities he described at University Park, Jimmy outlined his methods for making a church meaningful and vibrant to its members and to the community it served:

- To get participation in a church activity it has to be well-planned, and it has to mean something to the participants. If a program isn't meaningful, change it or eliminate it. There must be practical life applications for what is taught. For example, don't just study missionaries, learn from them and practice techniques they used.

- Wednesday night services are important and must be kept interesting and meaningful. Brother Jimmy's Wednesday programs were varied: sometimes a short sermon, sometimes Bible study, or testimonies. There was always time for prayer requests. Often he divided the congregation into small groups and scattered them throughout the church to pray, reminiscent of Sunday mornings at Steep Hollow when each Sunday school class took a corner of the little frame church.

- Deacons are spiritual leaders who assist the pastor in ministering to the congregation. They are not a governing body or a board of directors. Each deacon should be a tither and active soul-winner. The church council plans church programs. Good leadership on the council is essential. The council should plan church activities a year in advance, but with flexibility to accommodate last-minute opportunities and emergencies.

- Revivals are important for spiritual growth. Jimmy planned two each year at University Park and some years tried to hold three. He believed in "securing the best possible evangelists and singers." Jimmy himself conducted three or four revivals a year outside his church with the church's support.

- Growing churches will be in debt, but the amount of debt should never become burdensome. Draper's church in San Antonio financed its $175,000 expansion with $140,000 in bonds. They also supported missions. "Every church should have a mission all the time," he wrote. "Missions at home and abroad are the lifeblood of the church."

Jimmy still felt his true calling was in a "pioneer area," whether the frontier was geographic, economic, or cultural. He sensed a special burden for his revivals in Detroit and other urban centers outside the South. In the mid-1960s when integrated congregations were still a novelty, University Park–reflecting the integrated nature of the armed services–welcomed a number of black members during Jimmy's pastorate.

Jimmy also had a heart for mission churches reaching out to new communities and the unchurched. And so when the Lord finally led him to leave San Antonio it was for a church that was exactly that: a mission. It offered no prestige and no big jump in attendance or budget. In fact, by some earthly measures it was a step down–nothing like the obvious elevation in status and visibility a big church would bestow. But Brother Jimmy never did measure success or opportunity with statistics.

To him, opportunity came in the spring of 1965 from a struggling mission church in far-off Kansas City, Missouri, whose previous minister had taped a note to the door and left for good in the middle of the night.

CHAPTER 9

IN A STRANGE LAND

L UTHER DYER, pastor of Bethany Baptist Church in Kansas City, Missouri, was looking for some help. Bethany had established a mission church, Red Bridge Baptist Mission, and was struggling to keep it open. In a phone call to Brother Jimmy, Dyer explained that the mission had about 125 members but no pastor. A small, leaderless mission congregation hundreds of miles from anyplace Jimmy or any of his family ever lived—on the surface it was scarcely a career move worth considering. Yet deep down, something in the situation resonated inside Jimmy's heart, and he listened to the rest of the story.

The Red Bridge Mission, on the south side of Kansas City, was organized in 1963 as an outreach of Bethany to the local community. Over the next couple of years the congregation grew gradually under the leadership of a pastor they all loved and appreciated. That love was sorely tested when, not long before Christmas 1964, the pastor left a note for his flock on the door and moved away without warning in the middle of the night.

Piecing the story together later, the shocked and angry members deduced that their pastor panicked in the face of bad news about his son's health. The boy had asthma, and his doctor had warned the family that he needed to move to a healthier climate. One night the boy suffered a severe asthma attack. In the fear and desperation of the moment, the pastor packed up his family on the spot, stuck a note on the church treasurer's front door, and headed for Arizona. He contacted the church later to explain what happened and offer an apology, but the people were left unexpectedly without a leader.

Jimmy had not felt led to visit any of the churches expressing an interest in him during his years in San Antonio. Somehow this one was different. After a time of prayer and talking it over with Carol Ann, Jimmy went to Kansas City and preached at Bethany with the pulpit committee in attendance. The committee, with members from both Bethany and the Red Bridge mission, invited Jimmy back to preach at Red Bridge in view of a call. Accompanied this time by Carol Ann, Jimmy returned to Kansas City for another sermon and a closer look at life in the Midwest.

The signs were not promising. The former pastor's sudden exit had demoralized both the church and the mission. The congregation felt their trust had been betrayed, and some of them would have a hard time making any sort of emotional investment in a new man. The mission was divided and dispirited. They had trouble agreeing on anything. To Carol Ann it looked like "they would have split the vote over whether it was daylight or dark."

Flying home to San Antonio the couple sat side by side on the plane, lost in thought. After a silence Carol Ann turned to her husband and said more as a statement than a question, "Hon, there's no reason for us to come up here, is there?"

"No," Jimmy answered, "not at all. We have a wonderful, loving church right where we are. We're doing the Lord's work there. And besides—we don't have any of the winter clothes we'd need in Missouri!" In the days that followed, the talk turned from what they were and weren't doing, and what they did and didn't have in San Antonio, to what the Lord would have them do with their lives. Jimmy felt his burden for "pioneer areas"; there was definitely a pioneer spirit, as well as a pioneer element of risk, in accepting a call to Red Bridge.

After all the thinking and praying and pondering on any decision, the time eventually comes to throw away the arguments for and against and say, "OK, Lord, what is your will for our lives in this?" For the Drapers, when the time eventually came, they knew beyond any doubt that God was calling them to Red Bridge.

In May 1965, Brother Jimmy and his family—Carol Ann; seven-year-old Randy; Bailey, five; and Terri, who just turned four—said good-bye to their church and their home in San Antonio and headed north to Missouri.

It was the first time any of the Drapers had ever lived outside the South, and the first several months carried a heavy dose of culture shock. All their lives Jimmy and Carol Ann had spoken a friendly greeting to strangers, waved to neighbors on the street, dropped in on acquaintances for impromptu visits, and expected a steady stream of visitors in their own house. That Southern hospitality they took so much for granted was nonexistent there.

People kept to themselves, and no one seemed interested in making friends. Because the mission congregation was so divided and unsettled, it seemed impossible that Jimmy's call (or anyone else's) could be unanimous, and that members who thought the new pastor had been forced on them would be unhappy about it. Almost miraculously, there was only one negative vote.

In spite of this promising show of support, Carol Ann and Jimmy spent a lot of time praying for guidance and reassurance. The Red Bridge congregation bought a new parsonage much nicer than the little bungalow next to the church, but the early days there were still a time of adjustment and loneliness. Carol Ann wrote asking her mother not to put a stamp on her next letter. That way the postman would have to come to the door and collect the postage, and at least she would get to talk to somebody for a minute during the day. As lonely as she felt sometimes, there were always things to do with the children, and a constant sense of listening for God's will in the moment. It wasn't that the mission congregation had singled her out for the silent treatment; she soon realized that they didn't like each other either.

In spite of the tension, Jimmy attacked the challenges of his new position with all the energy he had. Though the attitude among the congregation remained flinty, Jimmy's genuineness and the love for people that flowed through his sermons began to bring people around. By the time Red Bridge was constituted as an independent church in October 1965, less than five months after Jimmy came as pastor, there were 350 charter members on the roll. And the growth continued at a pace Jimmy knew was one of God's miracles.

Carol Ann sensed the moment when the tide turned. It was the night the church was officially constituted. During the invitation at the end of the service a woman came down front and asked Brother Jimmy if she could speak. He escorted her to the microphone and she said, "God did good getting our pastor." There was a smattering of applause, the nodding of heads, and a chorus of "Amen!"

She went on: "And he is the pastor that we need. All of us have said things we shouldn't have said and listened to things we shouldn't have listened to. I think it's high time we pour out of the pews and give him the support he deserves."

To Carol Ann it seemed like at that instant "the Holy Spirit opened the windows, ushered Satan out, closed the windows, and began to abide in our midst. People began to get right with one another." Everyone in church who heard the woman's words that Sunday night streamed out of the pews to come down front, shake Brother Jimmy's hand and make him welcome. Carol Ann and the children were left alone in their seats watching the entire church being transformed in front of them. From that night on, the whole atmosphere was different, and the church grew at a rate nothing short of miraculous.

The Drapers' home was a roomy, modern, four-bedroom house. None of the children had ever seen a basement before, and were fascinated with it. The house was on a gentle slope, which allowed for a daylight basement with a walk-out door on the downhill side. They learned to listen for the sound of the tornado warning, which was their signal to run giggling down the base-ment steps (though providentially a tornado never came).

So far from familiar places and traditions, family ties took on a new level of importance in Jimmy's life. His three children were in school and acclimating quickly to their new surroundings, as children always seem to do. Both his brothers were in college, with George ambling along on his way to an undergraduate degree in eight years, and young Charlie taking the opposite tack, entering college after his junior year in high school to come within a year of graduating with his older brother.

Their father was now pastor of First Baptist Church in Warren, Arkansas. Ever the prolific correspondent, Jimmy seemed to write longer and more frequent letters to him than ever. In addition to the joys and woes of family foibles and politics, the James T. Drapers Junior and Senior traded thoughts about denominational matters, travel plans, and sermon topics and techniques.

James Senior had a fifteen-minute radio show from time to time which he enjoyed for the chance it gave him to bring the gospel to a newer and wider audience than he had preached to before. In one letter he exulted, "I don't recall being happier any time during my ministry. Your mother and I are both extremely happy, and the Lord is blessing the work in a fine way."

A typed note from the older pastor, dated March 17, 1966, was filled with enthusiasm and plans for the future. Though his health had been delicate for years, he was playing golf and feeling fine:

"Your phone call today did us as much good as a high-powered prescription. Thank you so much! Attached are the copies of the sermon notes . . . . The idea I got from one of Clovis Chappell's sermons. Under separate cover I am mailing the book to you. You may keep it until we rendezvous in Dallas [at the annual Convention] in June. Don't keep it any longer, on penalty of being burned at the stake. . . ."

Five days later, James Senior had lunch with the Rotarians in Warren and then joined them at the local country club for nine holes of golf. It was a revival week at his church with a busy schedule of events, which made a midweek retreat to the golf course even more welcome than usual. During the round, the elder Draper suddenly collapsed unconscious and was rushed to the hospital. He had had a heart attack. Within minutes he was dead at the age of fifty-two.

By the time Jimmy got to his mother's house it was already crowded with people coming to see her and pay their respects. All the activity and momentum of revival week was suddenly redirected at helping Lois Draper and her sons deal with so sudden and tragic a loss.

The parsonage in Warren was a big, rambling antebellum house with tall ceilings, large rooms, and a thirty-five step staircase. The street out front was jammed with cars, and the inside packed with stunned friends and church members there to offer condolences and do whatever they could. A visitor might have expected Mrs. Draper to be sitting solemnly on the couch in the parlor receiving her company. That wasn't her style. Instead she was going serenely from room to room comforting her friends on the loss of their pastor.

Jimmy and his brothers conducted their father's funeral. "God gave George, Charlie, and me the grace and strength to conduct the service," Jimmy wrote shortly afterwards, "and we feel it was a fitting climax to an outstanding life. Each of us feels that Daddy is living on in the thousands of things we discover in our lives each day that are just him. How blessed we have been to have the finest father and mother in all the world . . . and we will be with them again, perhaps soon, in God's eternal day!"

In the weeks that followed, Jimmy considered how best to settle his father's affairs and help his mother establish a new role and a new life for herself. Jimmy's father had never made a high salary, and his mother had never worked outside the home—raising three sons, being a pastor's wife, and enduring the lifelong effects of polio were surely work enough. Her widow's pension wasn't nearly sufficient to live on. Far from being able to assist her, sons George, 24, and Charlie, 18, were not financially self-sufficient themselves.

Without hesitation or the least sense of being burdened by this turn of events, Jimmy soon made arrangements for his mother to move in with him in Kansas City. His brothers were with them off and on as well. Charlie lived with them that summer, preached occasionally at Red Bridge when Jimmy was away, and held revivals in Texas. George prepared for both his wedding and his senior year at college in Marshall, Texas, with sights set on a teaching career.

Of course, there were adjustments as the far-flung family merged into one household. Charlie had started smoking during his first year at college and expected he might continue with the habit under Jimmy's roof. Jimmy had other plans. Seeing his youngest brother light up in the house, he motioned him outside and got straight to the point as only a brother could:

"If I ever see you smoking in here again after today I'm going to beat the stuffings out of you."

To his credit, Charlie quit cold turkey on the spot.

To Randy, Bailey, and Terri, it wasn't a chore having Grandmother and their uncle in the house, it was an adventure. Grandmother had her own room, and Charlie lived in the basement. Jimmy and Carol Ann assumed the responsibility for their financial and emotional welfare without missing a beat. Jimmy soon became a father figure to his younger brothers; his mother lived with them for the rest of her long life. Her being there through the years the children were growing up gave Jimmy and Carol Ann freedom to minister in ways they could never have done otherwise.

The Draper house became busier than ever, and the result wasn't frantic–it was fun. Not every widow would have been able to live so contentedly under her son's roof; not every wife would have welcomed her mother-in-law so suddenly and permanently; not every family of young children would have enjoyed sharing their house and their parents with two other generations of relatives. But the Drapers thanked God for the opportunity. Having the children grow up with their grandmother in the house was a rare blessing in a time when families were becoming more and more scattered.

Jimmy and Carol Ann extended their hospitality beyond the family. Two teenagers the family had mentored in San Antonio came to Kansas City and moved in for a while. Missionaries, church visitors, friends of friends, and anyone else were welcome anytime, and the extra beds were always made up. Carol Ann claimed the food might not be haute cuisine, but there was plenty of it.

Some of the young single ladies at church met a door-to-door magazine salesman who was down on his luck. They told him if he ever needed any help to call them. Once the phone in the Draper house rang at one in the morning. The salesmen had called one of the girls at church, and the girl called the pastor. The salesman was at the Kansas City bus station and needed a place to spend the night. Jimmy sent Charlie to pick him up, gave him a bed for the night, and fed him breakfast the next day, and the next, and the next. The "overnight" stay stretched to six weeks, until the day he borrowed $500 from a church member, then disappeared for good.

Jimmy's hospitality and compassion led him to sponsor two other prison inmates for release. The experience with Dean Foster in San Antonio hadn't worked out like Jimmy had prayed it would, and he hoped this time would be different. He sponsored Ray Summers, an inmate from the penitentiary in Vienna, Illinois, and moved him into a house on church property. It wasn't long before he, too, received visitors who lured him back to the criminal underworld. He left for Chicago but returned, seeming for a while to escape the pull of his criminal friends.

The friends were insistent and kept visiting. Jimmy received ominous phone calls for trying to shield Summers, then threats were made on Jimmy's life. The police began watching the house; officers escorted the children to school to head off any kidnapping attempt. Ray insisted that Jimmy let him look under his car every morning for bombs.

The ex-con also had a solution to the trouble. Of course Summers knew who was behind the threats. "I can take care of everything if you want me to," he promised. "You just say the word, and he's done!" Jimmy said he hoped there was another way to take care of things.

In the end Ray Summers's life ended tragically. He was found alone, dead of a gunshot wound. Officially the death was ruled accidental, that Summers had been cleaning a pistol when it went off. Jimmy always felt otherwise. The man knew too much about guns to shoot himself accidentally, and Jimmy had heard him say more than once, "I'd kill myself before I'd disappoint you or the church." It was a reminder to Jimmy of the unexplainable evil in the world and the truth that sometimes things happen that none of us can understand.

The other prisoner was a man named Sammy who was dying of cancer. Authorities had ruled the man could be released in order to live his last days out of prison, and asked Jimmy if they could release the man into his custody. Jimmy agreed that as long as Sammy's medical expenses were covered, he would be responsible for him otherwise.

Sammy was paroled to a hospital in Kansas City, where Jimmy and others visited him almost every day, sharing their testimonies and teaching him about Jesus. In time Sammy was saved and wanted to be baptized. With approval from both the hospital and the church, Jimmy and two other men from Red Bridge baptized Sammy in a hospital bathtub. It was one of the most touching and heartfelt services Jimmy ever conducted. It was also the last time Sammy ever left his bed. A few days later he peacefully passed away.

Jimmy's hand of Christian friendship extended to family, strangers, and criminals alike. The same drive made him a strong believer in visitation. He loved going to homes, sharing the gospel with people, and inviting them to church. It was, after all, a family tradition. The last three years of his life, Jimmy's father, accompanied by Mrs. Draper, visited literally thousands of people a year in a town of five thousand, in spite of their chronic health problems.

The first months at Red Bridge, visitations had been hard because the atmosphere in the church was still so divisive. Jimmy and Carol Ann started at ten o'clock Saturday morning and visited all day. It was good to share the gospel with others, but it was a challenge to get fired up about inviting anyone to a church where the people argued with one another. Once the church was constituted and the air was cleared, visitation became more comfortable, and church attendance surged.

By the end of 1966, under Jimmy's leadership, Red Bridge led all the Southern Baptist churches in Missouri in baptisms and was "desperately in need of additional building." They were first statewide in baptisms again in 1967, and once more in 1968. People were inspired by the message of Jimmy's sermons and the conviction he showed in preaching them. Most critical of all to the growth of the church was Jimmy's ability to make everyone feel special and important.

He instituted the Prayergram, a yellow sheet of note paper that looked like a telegram, and encouraged church members to use them for notes of praise and encouragement to one another, or to say they were praying for them or thinking about them. Hundreds of Prayergrams went back and forth every month, some hand delivered at church, others mailed to members' homes, and more sent to members and visitors out of town. Whenever Jimmy preached out of town, some were mailed to him at the church he was visiting and many more awaited him when he returned.

No matter how busy he got, Brother Jimmy took care not to slight his family. His wife and children were an inspiration and a blessing to him, and he studiously avoided inducing the common preacher's kid complaint that "Daddy's never home." When he was away he wrote Carol Ann almost every day. She wrote him too, and took dictation from each of the children, adding their messages to her own.

When his oldest child, Randy, turned ten, Jimmy wrote a letter to him that was a tender expression of the breadth and depth of the Christian experience, and an insight into his own spiritual journey:

Randy, I want to share some things with you very simply. You'll not understand all of them now, but I want you to put this letter where you can read it again in the years ahead.

Firstly, my son, never forget that the only meaningful and happy life is found in Jesus Christ. Get to know Him better. Walk with Him—talk with Him daily. Your life will always be just wonderful as He lives in your heart. . . .

Secondly, always be true to your call from God. Never forget that He has placed His hand on you. Remember 2 Tim. 2:15 ["Be diligent to present yourself approved to God, a worker who doesn't need to be ashamed, correctly teaching the word of truth."] and always do your best in school. . . . It's no disgrace or sin to be average or to fail in an attempt to do something. It is wrong when you've not done your best.

Thirdly, remember that you represent Christ in everything you do. When you are playing ball, sitting in church, listening in school, doing chores around the house or playing with Bailey and Terri you are showing to everyone what a Christian is like! Do it right, Randy. Always tell the truth. Always be polite. Always play fair. Always have a smile. Always consider the other person. Never return spite for spite. Never be ugly to someone just because they have been ugly to you! . . .

Finally, remember that your daddy is called of God to preach the wonderful gospel of Jesus Christ. That is my life. It is more important to me than life itself. It is not easy for me, nor will it be easy for you. Your grand-daddy was a preacher too, so I know what it is like to have a preacher father. There will be many times when I won't be able to be with you even though it is what I want more than anything. Helping people is my calling from God and it takes me away from home many times. You will hear some people very harshly criticize me. That is to be expected because the Devil wants to keep me from serving God effectively. Don't be surprised or upset when you hear such things. God is in control of life and our world and He will take care of things like that. Just know that everything I try to do is for Christ's glory. . . .

I am proud to be your father. May God add many more wonderful years to your life is my prayer and may your life always bring honor to Him. Happy Birthday, son.

Communication on paper, in the pulpit, and in person continued as one of Jimmy's strongest attributes. He took the same diligence in answering a letter from a child as he did writing a prominent deacon or community leader, and he responded to both equally promptly. He personally answered every letter he received and returned every phone call. He remembered people's names and the names of their children. A frequent comment was that when Brother Jimmy was talking to you, you were the only person in the world to him. Whatever else was going on in the church or around the office, when you were talking to him, you had his undivided attention. Public officials or custodians, children or millionaires, Brother Jimmy treated them all alike.

To Jimmy Draper, good communication was as natural as breathing; he considered it part of his calling. Yet his level of connection and commitment to others was extraordinary; it was one of a range of God-given gifts that were preparing him for still greater opportunities.

CHAPTER 10

RED BRIDGE
AND REVOLUTION

A T THE SAME TIME Jimmy was building Red Bridge into one
of Missouri's most noteworthy congregations, he was
achieving a higher profile in the denomination than ever before.
The success at Red Bridge had something to do with his success
as a pastor, but Jimmy also excelled at other tasks the Lord gave
him to do. Without any active politicking on his part, Jimmy
began moving deeper into the network of influential Baptist leaders and higher up the ladder of denominational responsibility.

Luther Dyer, pastor of Bethany Baptist Church when its mission at Red Bridge called Jimmy, became state evangelism director. This high-profile position required him to organize or attend
conferences, revivals, and other events across Missouri. Since he
had seen the fruit of Jimmy's labor at Red Bridge first hand,
he invited him to participate in many of these activities. Speaking
and preaching at these gatherings exposed Jimmy to a wider audience. Jimmy's colleague and friend Al Metzger formed the first

city-wide Youth for Christ organization in Kansas City, introducing Jimmy to another network of partners in ministry.

In 1967 Billy Graham scheduled a crusade in Kansas City as part of his Mid-America Crusade and, as he always did, prepared the way with the help of a steering committee of local pastors and community leaders. Graham wanted a Southern Baptist on the executive committee, which consisted of twenty or so men in charge. After the work of the committee was under way the Baptist member left. The Billy Graham Crusade staff wanted another Baptist to take his place, and Jimmy Draper was recommended for the position. (Perhaps the invitation reminded Draper of his first meeting with Graham fourteen years before, when he and his friend Charles Dan Olgesby were escorting Roy Rogers and Dale Evans across the field at Rice Stadium.)

What Draper didn't know at first was that the Baptist who left the executive committee was also the prayer chairman. This was a very public position that required Jimmy to assume responsibility for a fifteen-minute radio program every day during the month before the Crusade. Jimmy taped the show at a studio every morning, and it aired on a top station in a prime 10 a.m. slot, right after *Dear Abby*. The same genuineness and love for people that brought new members to Red Bridge came through on the radio too. The broadcasts introduced Jimmy to thousands of new listeners—some who used his teaching to affirm their own beliefs, and others who had never given Christianity a second thought but were intrigued by this exuberant and confident voice that came on after *Dear Abby*, following her down-to-earth advice with Christ's good news about everlasting life.

In January 1968, Luther Dyer invited Jimmy to address the Missouri Baptist Evangelism Conference in Jefferson City. Dyer's thank-you letter indicated that Draper's success in reaching his audience of pastors and executives equaled his success on the radio:

"I have never been so proud of anyone in my entire life. Your message to Missouri Baptists was just what the Holy Spirit ordered. . . . Once again I say that my claim to fame is the fact that I had a part in bringing James T. Draper, Jr., to the great State of Missouri."

Early that spring Jimmy accepted an invitation from Jack Cousins of the Billy Graham organization to speak at a pastors conference in San Antonio. The meeting was held in advance of a crusade planned for the city during HemisFair, a gigantic world's fair then under way that had been years in the planning. Jimmy's challenge was to get the pastors enthused about the Crusade and convince them to promote it to their congregations.

After the conference, Cousins was convinced that Draper's presentation was what got the momentum going. He wrote, "I don't know how to express my thanks to you for coming to San Antonio. I believe the Lord used you here to spark the Crusade. I felt it was one of the finest challenges I've ever heard to present the program. We have seen the results of this message in the splendid cooperation we have been receiving since then. . . . We needed this to break through and just get the ball in motion. I believe God is going to give us a great harvest."

The harvest continued at home too. Brother Jimmy led a building program at Red Bridge, making plans and raising money to build a new sanctuary to hold the members and visitors that now packed the old building several times a week. The church budget topped $100,000 a year for the first time ever.

Growth was not without its challenges, of course. The chairman of the trustees at Red Bridge resigned, citing his dissatisfaction with the way expenses were approved. Brother Jimmy's response was a conciliatory letter that retraced every step of the misunderstanding in detail, explaining the way the approval structure was set up and how it was followed. In the end, Jimmy humbly assumed responsibility for the breach: "I admire you and respect you more than words can tell. It grieves me that I have so failed you that your actions regarding the budget pledge and trustees were necessary."

Such situations were rare. Almost to a person, everyone who set foot in Red Bridge Baptist Church loved Jimmy Draper.

One July Sunday, Brother Jimmy and his family came into the sanctuary and saw a special display on the altar table with a globe and maps. Carol Ann thought there might be a program about missions coming up. Before the service was over the secret was revealed: it was a special program all right, but it was one of thanksgiving for the Drapers' ministry. To thank and honor their pastor and his wife, Red Bridge staged a Christmas in July celebration. Their gift to them was a Christmastime trip to the Holy Land, all expenses paid.

Jimmy could scarcely imagine being singled out like that for doing what he thought was no more than his duty and calling as a pastor. It seemed too extravagant a gift at first, until Jimmy reminded himself of something his father had said: "Let people do things for you if they want to." As well as being a gracious host, Brother Draper was also a gracious guest.

Christmas that year found Jimmy and Carol Ann in Jerusalem, out of the country for the first time in their lives on an adventure they would never forget.

The first memorable moment was landing in Paris and finding all the airport workers on strike. There was no food or any other kind of passenger services. After hours in a temporary waiting area without water or heat, Jimmy and Carol Ann caught a flight to Tel Aviv and finally arrived in Jerusalem after midnight.

Jimmy's first glance out his hotel window the next morning made it all worthwhile. A panorama of the Old City stretched out below; in the foreground was a man walking beside a donkey cart. It was as though he had been suddenly transported back to the time of Jesus. Within a week he saw the spot by the Sea of Galilee where Jesus may have sat to deliver the Sermon on the Mount; the dungeon believed to be the site where Jesus was kept prisoner in the house of the high priest; and the hillside steps where Jesus probably walked from the upper room to the Garden of Gethsemane. Tracing those steps brought Jimmy to tears.

He thought that in some ways he learned more during a week in Jerusalem than he learned in seminary. The history of Christianity made sense in a way it never had before. He was surprised at how much closer it brought him to the person of Jesus.

And by the time they got home, there was another surprise waiting.

Back in January 1968 Jimmy had spoken with his friend John Bisagno about coming to preach or hold a revival at Red Bridge. Bisagno was pastor of First Southern Baptist Church of Del City, Oklahoma, a close-in suburb on the southeast side of Oklahoma City. In his reply to the invitation, John wrote to Brother Jimmy, "Please keep this under your hat, but at this moment something big may be in the wind that will greatly change my future schedule."

Of course there were always rumors and suppositions floating around about when and where a particular pastor might receive a call from a pulpit committee. Jimmy evidently thought no more about his friend's mysterious allusion.

Within days after Jimmy and Carol Ann returned to Kansas City from Jerusalem, they left again for a state evangelism conference in

Saint Louis. Between presentations at the conference, Jimmy's friend and colleague Dick Cole came over and sat down in the row in front of Jimmy and Carol Ann. Dick was pastor of First Baptist Church in Raytown, a large Kansas City congregation.

"Are you packed yet?" Dick asked.

"You mean are we *unpacked* yet? From our trip to Israel?" Jimmy responded.

"No, are you packed to move to Del City?"

"What are you talking about?"

"John Bisagno's leaving for First Baptist Church, Houston, and you're going to be the new pastor."

Jimmy chuckled. "I haven't heard a word from any pulpit committee."

True, he hadn't been contacted officially, but friends in the church had been in touch. Don Demeter, a deacon and member of the pulpit committee, was a former major league baseball player who once hit three home runs in a single World Series game. Mike Brumley, rookie All-Star catcher with the Washington Senators (later the Texas Rangers), was an evangelist and church member. The two of them had called Brother Jimmy earlier and said, "Have you prayed about Del City?" The church was looking for Bisagno's replacement. "I haven't really thought about it," Jimmy answered, joking, "Do you sign with a team before you have a contract?"

Bisagno knew that as an evangelist, Mike Brumley worked closely with pastors all over the country. When the process of finding Bisagno's successor began, he asked Brumley, "Who is the best pastor you've ever worked with?" The quick answer was, "Jimmy Draper."

The next Sunday, a few weeks before Bisagno was scheduled to leave Del City for Houston, the Del City pulpit committee came to hear Jimmy Draper in Kansas City. It could scarcely have been a more miserable experience for Brother Jimmy. He had played a hard-driving game of church basketball the night before. At two o'clock Sunday morning he woke up with a raging stomach virus. From then until the time came for him to leave for church, he lost eight pounds.

Pastor Jimmy arrived at Red Bridge that morning exhausted and pale, with big dark bags under his eyes. He couldn't imagine impressing a pulpit committee from a church more than twice the size of his own. After the service Jimmy met with the committee. It was an emotional time, with several men in tears as they prayed for God's guidance in the decision before them.

The following Thursday, Jimmy was with Luther Dyer in Sikeston, Missouri, holding one-day rallies for the Billy Graham crusade when the pulpit committee tracked him down and asked him to bring Carol Ann and come to Del City for an interview. He made the trip, and the committee asked him to come in view of a call. The church in Red Bridge was strong now, and the opportunity in Del City was compelling. It was a big church that offered Jimmy his biggest platform yet for sharing the gospel of Christ. Once again the job had sought the man; the man hadn't sought the job. When he felt sure God was calling him in that direction, he accepted the challenge. Soon the Drapers made the move to Oklahoma City and a new field of Christian service.

Del City had a reputation as one of the most evangelistic churches in the denomination. Many churches saw the popular culture of the 1960s as a threat. Traditional Christian morality and behavior had been the cultural norm for as long as anybody could remember; suddenly the definition of "normal" was under siege. Some churches saw themselves as fortresses against change. Del City, by contrast, threw its doors open wide to all comers.

The 1960s were watershed years for American Christianity in a way that Brother Jimmy had been somewhat protected from. His church in San Antonio had a high percentage of military families, and they tended to be relatively conservative. Red Bridge, at least in its earlier phase under Jimmy, was too preoccupied trying to resolve internal discord and keep the bills paid to fret much about the wider social picture (though they did vote to accept their first black members during Jimmy's pastorate). In Del City it all hit home that building a church in the aftermath of the cultural revolution of the 1960s required something new.

Oklahoma is a conservative, traditional-minded state. The appearance of hippies with their ragged clothes and unwashed bodies, "free love," iconoclastic music, and antiestablishment mind-set put plenty of Southern Baptist preachers on the offensive, delivering fiery sermons against long hair and short skirts. Del City was different and proudly so. The congregation there didn't bend an inch when it came to what the Bible said was right and wrong, but they welcomed everybody regardless of what they wore or what they smelled like. "They didn't condone sin or anti-Americanism," Jimmy said, "but the church was willing to do whatever it took to bring people to the gospel." (One other church in town eventually thought the Del City congregation drifted so far outside the mainstream that they took out a full-page newspaper ad condemning them.)

Jimmy continued the contemporary trend his predecessor in the pulpit had set, adding his own distinctive brand of personal evangelism, longstanding commitment to visitation, and the sincerity that shone in everything he said and did. A decade or more before it became commonplace in Southern Baptist churches, Del City had a praise band with electric guitars that performed pop gospel music in the services. The youth music combo, The

Revolution, gained local popularity and even made a record. Older members didn't like all the newfangled racket, but they accepted it because it proved to be an effective tool for bringing people to Christ who wouldn't have come to church otherwise. They were willing to focus on results and substance rather than appearance.

A few hard-core traditionalists insisted the integrity of Christianity was at stake. Even though these members condemned electric guitars and "mod" clothing, Jimmy Draper kept using them to spread the gospel. Noting how big public events could draw a crowd for evangelizing, Jimmy got the church to rent the coliseum in town and sponsor a concert by 1950s actor/singer/heartthrob and 1960s evangelist Pat Boone. Another time he rented an entire theme park for the day and invited the church and any interested visitors to join in Christian Family Day, ending with a worship service. Judging by the turnout, it was a tremendous success.

Jimmy also continued the Bisagno tradition of the Starlite Crusades every July, one of the most popular summer events in the community. It was a series of open-air revivals under the lights of the local high school football stadium. Five thousand people brought their lawn chairs—some brought picnics—and sat on the field, packing the stadium for a night of singing, preaching, witnessing, and decisions for Christ. There were families all over the state who planned their vacations around the Starlite Crusade.

It was too hot to dress up. Some attended in T-shirts and jeans. Others came in open-collared shirts, with a smattering of sport coats here and there in the audience. Ladies wore their cotton or linen summer dresses. A few younger couples and singles were decked out in tie-dyes. For many church families it was the highlight of the season.

Sometimes the informality of the Starlite Crusade made its way into the church on Sunday morning. Hippies came barefoot in their cutoffs and sat on the floor. Jimmy and the church allowed it; they just wanted to see people saved. Traditionally, church congregations don't applaud. The idea behind the custom is that whatever the musicians or speakers are doing in the worship service is to the glory of God, not for accolades like they would expect from an audience at a show. God gets the glory in the form of praise, rather than the performer getting it in the form of applause.

That sort of thinking went out the window at Del City. The new trend was to applaud, and the church didn't discourage it. In time they were applauding everything, including the announcements. Certainly the level of decorum was changed, but, as Jimmy said, "people were getting saved." Sometimes the congregation applauded during baptisms. One memorable night in particular when the youth pastor was baptizing a woman, she panicked at the last instant and grabbed him around the neck. He quickly assessed the situation, took a big breath, and went down with her. The congregation exploded in laughter, cheers, and applause. It wasn't an embarrassing moment—it was a joyful one. The people in that room loved each other, and they loved the Lord.

"Change is not an option," Brother Jimmy said in describing his ministry at Del City. "Change is inevitable. The best we can hope for is to manage change, not be victimized or marginalized by it. A good pastor keeps people from being threatened by change. A good pastor is a leader, not a driver. The people have to understand why changes are made. Del City was the best possible situation: I didn't lead them; they led me."

When the Drapers moved to Oklahoma they first lived in a rental house and then the Del City parsonage. A little later they moved again, into a house they built. For the children, one of the highlights of living in a house of their own was that they each got to choose the colors for their rooms. Randy picked a wild combination of purple, black, and blue; Bailey chose red, white, and blue; and Terri got bright yellow. Keeping the same iconoclastic flavor, Carol Ann painted several of the rooms a vibrant peach and one wall in the master bedroom black. In the use of vibrant interior design they were ahead of the times. It was a happy home and one they all loved.

Grandmother Lois made the move with them, and it wasn't long before Jimmy and the family welcomed friends and strangers alike to the "Draper Motel" as often as they had in Kansas City. Randy, Bailey, and Terri were used to all kinds of people living under their roof. When a new education director came to serve with Jimmy, he and his wife and three children lived with the Drapers for four months.

Another time a hippie couple lived and ate at the house for several days. The girl arrived at church "very pregnant," and later brought her baby home from the hospital to the Draper house. Parents and child lived and ate at the house for several weeks, then packed up one day and left for good, blessed by Christian hospitality and, Carol Ann hoped, touched in some way with the message of Christ's love for them.

Part of the reason the Drapers connected so easily with all types of people was that Jimmy and Carol Ann never took themselves too seriously. Jimmy wasn't the kind of pastor who remained aloof from the church. If a skit called for him to put a bandanna on his head and hold a big lollypop, that's what he did.

One episode of many showing Jimmy's love of a good time was when his friend Jack Taylor invited him back to San Antonio from Del City to preach a revival. The whole Draper family went for the event and stayed with the Taylors. Word got out that the young people of the church in San Antonio were going to wrap the Taylor house with toilet paper. The invaders arrived and began their assault, only to be counterattacked by Jack and Jimmy on the roof with garden hoses, and their kids jumping out from behind the bushes and trees with water balloons and shaving cream.

As pastor of Del City, Jimmy got invitations to speak from all over the country, "not because I was Jimmy Draper," he insisted, "but because I was pastor at Del City." This was another big jump in notoriety for Brother Jimmy. John Bisagno had left the church with the reputation as "the most evangelistic church in the SBC," with the tradition of Starlite Crusades and other attributes that made it a high-profile pastorate. Jimmy took this great church and made it even better: bigger, more influential, more capable of bringing the world to Christ. One Sunday morning alone there were sixty-eight professions of faith.

Three years into his pastorate at Del City he attracted the attention of another church. As at every previous crossroads in his career, Jimmy wasn't looking for a change. He often said he would gladly live out the rest of his life serving the Lord in Del City, and he meant it with all his heart. But now God had a new road in mind for Brother Jimmy, and for the first time in his career he was in for a rocky ride.

CHAPTER 11

THE PERILS OF SUCCESS

DEL CITY LOVED THE DRAPERS, and the feeling was mutual. Jimmy could see himself staying there for the rest of his life. The children loved Oklahoma, the church was growing at a record-setting clip, and Brother Jimmy was in ever-greater demand as a revivalist. With three teenagers in the household now there were always school activities to keep up with, plus church youth events, sports, music, and on and on.

It was a season of memorable family vacations to the Floyd grandparents in Lake Jackson, or to Colorado to visit Draper relatives for hiking and hunting. As Jimmy had done with his brothers and parents a generation before, they traveled by car, whiling away the hours on the road by telling stories, singing songs, and playing games. The trips were filled with fun and laughter; years later it was the laughter the children remembered most of all.

Jimmy led his family at play with the same enthusiasm he led his church at worship. He was ever mindful of how preachers' kids often felt neglected. A certain amount of business travel was unavoidable. But he was with his wife and children whenever it was possible; and when he was with them they had his undivided attention. For example, Terri loved walking in the Colorado countryside, so her father often walked with her. They carved their initials on a tree one summer, then returned to it several times on later trips.

While he was at Del City, Jimmy made his first foreign mission trip to Brazil and Argentina. It gave him a new perspective on evangelism and a fresh appreciation for the sacrifices missionaries made in the service of Christ. He arranged to call the church from South America during a Sunday night service, reporting on his activities and asking them for their prayers. He got a round of laughter and applause when out of the blue he said of his older son, "Whatever Randy's doing, tell him to quit it!"

In the three years following Brother Jimmy's arrival at Del City in 1970, the number of baptisms doubled and average weekly attendance went from 1,200 to 2,300. Jimmy kept steadily to his customary packed schedule of revivals, conferences, and denominational meetings. As in the past, he received feelers from other churches looking for a new pastor, but felt strongly that the Lord had more work for him in Oklahoma.

In the spring of 1973 Jimmy held a young adult retreat at First Baptist Church in Dallas. While he was there he preached Sunday morning at the invitation of the pastor, W. A. Criswell. The Dallas congregation had more than fourteen thousand members, making it one of the largest and most influential churches in America. Wallie Amos Criswell, an iconic figure among Southern Baptists, had come to lead the church as a young man in 1944 and spent almost thirty years in the pulpit there. During that time, First Baptist Dallas had broken out of the pack to become the superstar church in the denomination.

Dr. Criswell and the church leadership had begun to consider the question of Criswell's successor. One or two good men came on staff with the expectation of being groomed as the next senior pastor, but somehow the succession process was interrupted and the men left. There was no overt plan for Criswell to retire and have his replacement take over. The plain fact was, however, that Criswell was not in robust health, had a punishing schedule, and couldn't keep up the present pace indefinitely. He acknowledged that he was tired and wanted someone to help him lead the church and take an active role in day-to-day management. This arrangement, some church leaders believed, would become a formal succession plan in time.

Unofficially, the snag was Criswell himself. With God's help and guidance, he had built one of the most phenomenal churches in the country. The vast majority of his working life had been in service to First Baptist Dallas. Without it he would be adrift. Though he surely knew the importance and practicality of locking in a succession plan, he couldn't imagine handing over the reins of power.

One reason he couldn't turn loose may have been that in his heart Criswell hadn't met anyone he felt he could hand the reins over to; hadn't seen the pastor and leader who could manage such a huge and multifaceted enterprise. When he heard Jimmy Draper preach the Sunday after his weekend retreat for young adults, Criswell thought he had his man. He'd known Draper because of the prominent place Del City held in the denomination as an evangelistic vanguard. Seeing the results of the young adult retreat and hearing the preaching the next day, Criswell set the motion in process for inviting Brother Jimmy to become his associate pastor.

It was a hard decision to leave Del City. There Jimmy had built a church the same way Dr. Criswell had built First Baptist Dallas, though in only a fraction of the time and on a smaller scale. Another factor to consider was that he had been a pastor throughout his career, never an associate. "If it had been up to me," Carol Ann admitted years later, "I'd have said, 'No, thank you,' and hung up the phone." She thought, *Lord, if you send us there it'll be a joke on the whole world.* She knew, though, that if the Lord heard her husband's prayers He heard hers. The final decision was his, and Carol Ann had faith that God would never lead them in different paths. She joined Jimmy in prayers for guidance and, for the time being, kept her worries to herself.

Jimmy and Carol Ann traveled to Dallas to meet with the personnel committee, where Dr. Criswell praised him warmly and affirmed to the group in Jimmy's presence that some day he would turn the church over to him and that he would become the pastor. Jimmy made it clear that if he came to Dallas it would be as the associate pastor, with no official promises or expectations about the future. "I can't come on that basis as Dr. Criswell's successor," he explained. "The church has the right to call its own pastor. If I come, Dr. Criswell, I'll come to be your associate, to help. If the Lord opens up the door for me to stay later on, that's fine, but that's not the reason I'd come." That was the appropriate response. Even so, everybody in the room believed Draper was Criswell's hand-picked replacement because that was what Criswell told them. Deacon Del Rogers, who was on the personnel committee and present for that meeting, said concerning Jimmy's response, 'I respected you before that, but I loved you after that!'"

Friends of Jimmy who thought they knew Dr. Criswell better than he did argued against leaving Del City for Dallas. One of them, Doyle Sumrall, dropped everything and flew to Oklahoma City to try and talk Jimmy out of accepting the call as associate pastor. He felt it was a huge mistake. Jimmy appreciated the genuine concern, but ultimately had no doubt the Lord was calling him and his family to Dallas.

It was hard to say good-bye to Del City. Jimmy and the church had come so far together that it seemed like leaving a close relative or best friend behind. In advance of his departure the church hosted a Jimmy Draper Appreciation Day. The governor of Oklahoma signed a proclamation declaring a Jimmy Draper Day statewide. Iconoclastic, unconcerned with appearances, and on fire with the Holy Spirit, First Southern Baptist Church of Del City had a great future ahead under new leadership. And Jimmy seemed poised to take full command of First Baptist Dallas sooner rather than later.

The move from Del City to Dallas was a trying one for the family, especially for Randy, who was the first sophomore at his high school ever elected president of the student body and now faced spending his junior year as a stranger in a new high school instead. The typical Del City church member was middle-income and middle-class, partly blue-collar with a fair number of young counterculture types thrown in for leavening. By contrast the Dallas membership roll included dozens of millionaires and literally hundreds of nationally prominent businessmen. As a whole, the membership at Dallas cut across economic and social lines from one extreme to the other, but the decision-makers were decidedly affluent.

Previous moves left the Drapers with a combination of sadness and a sense of excitement. This one was different; there was an unaccountably ominous cast to it, as though this time God's calling and the Drapers' wishes were miles apart. Carol Ann thought,

I know this is God's will, though I'd like it not to be. Jimmy had conflicting feelings too, more than he'd ever had before. Everybody who knew him congratulated him and looked ahead to the day when he would take the helm in Dallas. No one deserved it more or had earned it more fully. To his friends and colleagues, this pastorate was the one God had been preparing him for all his life.

In his heart, Jimmy believed God had other plans. Carol Ann and the children moved to an apartment in Dallas in August of 1973 to get ready for the school year, while Jimmy stayed behind for several weeks to complete the transition in Del City. Finally moving day came, and the movers loaded up all the furniture from the colorful "Draper Del City Motel" and headed for Texas. Jimmy, accompanied by his brother Charlie, took one last walk through the empty house, a house designed by a former church member in Kansas City and built just for his family.

Charlie was proud of his older brother's new calling and could scarcely contain his excitement over the new Dallas position. With the two of them alone in the house, Charlie gave voice to the thought shared by many. "You're going to be pastor there before long."

He repeated the prediction, expecting an answering expression of excitement or affirmation. Suddenly Jimmy turned and faced his brother, eyes intent, his jaw clenched.

"I will never be pastor at Dallas!"

Charlie, a seminary graduate and pastor himself, was shocked speechless. After a moment he found his voice. "Why on earth would you leave a ministry like Del City if you thought that?"

"I know what Dr. Criswell and others told me, but I'll never be pastor there."

"Why are you going?"

There was a long pause as Jimmy looked for the words, then, "The only thing I can tell you is that the Lord wants me to help Dr. Criswell." He was uncertain of everything except the most essential certainty of all: that this was God's will.

Jimmy joined the family in September and moved into a house in Dallas. Draper quickly assumed the role as the executive officer of his new church. He and Dr. Criswell presided jointly at meetings with the deacons—a body numbering more than three hundred in all. Draper managed the office and took responsibility for everything regarding the operation of the church and the ministry. At the senior pastor's request, he read and answered Criswell's mail as well as his own.

Jimmy preached every Sunday night and on Sunday mornings when asked or in Dr. Criswell's absence. His sermons were fresh and inspiring, infused with the evangelistic fervor of Del City but with a grounding in biblical teaching that gave them an air of authority. The services were broadcast live on KRLD radio, one of the oldest and most powerful stations in the South with coverage over the whole region.

Jimmy became immensely popular. Attendance at Sunday night worship surged under his leadership to the point where there was discussion about going to two evening services for the first time ever. Giving to the church increased, and weekly attendance regularly topped five thousand. Relieved of the burdens of day-to-day management, correspondence, and evening preaching, Dr. Criswell found more time to write, travel, and prepare the flagship Sunday morning messages that had helped build his reputation over the decades. One day he told Draper privately, "Lad, you've given me ten years of my life back."

By the summer of 1975 Jimmy had assumed other high-profile responsibilities in the denomination. He was a trustee of the

Southern Baptist Annuity Board and a trustee of his alma mater, Baylor University. His position as associate pastor at such an important church and his demonstrated success as a leader and manager made him a visible and valuable addition to these trustee boards.

The first sign of trouble at First Baptist Dallas came when Draper and Criswell were traveling home together from the 1975 Southern Baptist Convention in Miami. The topic of succession came up, as it did from time to time, and Criswell said something that took Brother Jimmy by surprise: "If the church were to vote to call you as pastor today, 98 percent of them would vote yes. But the other 2 percent are so vocal they'll never let it happen."

Jimmy always insisted he would pastor at Dallas only after a formal call just as any candidate would receive, not as a pre-arranged "promotion" from associate pastor. As popular as Jimmy undeniably was and as much as everyone seemed to love him and his family, the notion that a small group would circumvent the will of the majority absolutely astonished him. But it wasn't a complete surprise.

Brother Jimmy knew that associate pastors had come on staff previously with the expectation of succeeding Dr. Criswell, only to get crosswise somehow and leave. He also knew, if he was completely honest with himself, that there was a faction at First Baptist Dallas that was aggressively protective of Dr. Criswell's legacy and irrationally jealous of anyone who threatened it.

Dr. Criswell knew about it too, because its leader was his wife.

It wasn't something people talked about openly—then or thirty years later—but according to insiders in a position to know fully what was going on, Betty Criswell held a position of great influence over her husband and his church from behind the scenes. Mrs. Criswell's power base was rooted in the four-hundred-member Sunday school class she taught each week. It included some of the wealthiest and most powerful members of the church, men and women who shared Mrs. Criswell's desire to see Dr. Criswell's light shine unchallenged. Some deacons were a part of this group and some weren't, leading to the formation of various political factions within the deacon body.

Though his wife was most active in stirring up what discontent she could over Brother Jimmy, Criswell inadvertently undercut Draper's authority. One extreme case involved a staff member the personnel committee wanted dismissed. She was the wedding planner and director of singles activities, past seventy and clearly unable to do her job any longer. Draper reported to Criswell that the personnel committee thought she should go. Criswell had a soft spot for the woman because she had helped him raise his only child, a daughter, and was a long-time friend of the family.

"If you don't want to do this, we won't do it," Draper assured Criswell.

"Oh no, Lad," Criswell answered. "If that's the way you all feel, that's what we'll do."

"Just don't tell me yes and then change your mind."

"No, no, you go ahead."

With the personnel committee's endorsement, Jimmy announced her retirement, hosted a party for her, and gave her a big color television. Then the Saturday before her last Sunday, Criswell called his associate, admitting, "Ah, Lad, I just can't do it. I just can't do it."

Dumbfounded as he was, Draper remained loyal and respectful—and also honest. "Pastor, that's OK," he said. "I just want you to realize you've made it impossible for me to do my job. You told me to do this, I did it the way you told me to do it, and now you're

121

saying you're not going to stand by it. You're the pastor, and I honor that. But you've made it impossible for me to do my job."

In the summer of 1975 Dr. and Mrs. Criswell went to Europe for two months' vacation, and Jimmy preached every Sunday morning and night. The church was packed; members and visitors alike crowded in to hear Draper's sermons. Mrs. Criswell's friends told her that Brother Jimmy was out to get her husband's job, "out to steal Dr. Criswell's church from him" as the buzz went. In their view he was tooting his own horn while the senior pastor was away, trying to score promotion points and have Dr. Criswell shunted aside.

By the time the Criswells returned, charges and counter-charges were bouncing around among the membership about Draper and his motives. Jimmy and Carol Ann took the family on summer vacation near the end of the season, leaving town on a Monday, the day before the Criswells flew in from London. Later that week, the chairman of the personnel committee, a dear friend of Brother Draper's, tracked him down by phone to say the committee had met with Criswell. They reported that the summer he was away was the best summer the church had ever had, with the auditorium packed day and night and income at an all-time high.

Enthusiastically the committee chairman said, "Jimmy, you're more in the saddle than you've ever been!"

When he hung up the phone, Draper looked at his wife and said simply, "It's over."

Later in the summer, Draper got an unexpected glimpse of the true lay of the land when, taking their conversation off on a sudden tangent, Criswell turned to his associate and asked, "Why is Mrs. C. so opposed to you?"

"Pastor, do you really want to know?" Jimmy answered.

"Yes."

"She thinks I'm a threat to you."

Criswell sat stone-still. His face reddened. "That's an insult to me!" He paused for a moment, then nodded his head. "But you're right. That's what she thinks."

"Pastor, I'm no threat to you," Jimmy insisted. "I don't want to take anything from you. I'm happy to be your associate and do whatever you need done." But the conversation was a reality check that further jolted Draper into the realization that his time in Dallas was growing short.

At the same time this was going on, the church personnel committee insisted to Brother Jimmy that his elevation to the pastorate was only a matter of time. The two years since his arrival had been the most fruitful in the church's history, they said, and First Baptist Dallas was flourishing as never before. The credit, they believed, could largely be attributed to Jimmy's efforts. The committee commended his loyalty and humility in not responding to accusations that he was after the pastor's job.

They said that in fact they eventually expected him to become their pastor with the church's blessing. But by this time Brother Jimmy could no longer envision himself in that position; he would never allow himself to become a divisive force in one of the denomination's greatest congregations.

He later recalled, "I thought about it for about thirty seconds, then I said, 'I will not go down in history as the man who split First Baptist Dallas.'" Within three months the Drapers moved to Euless.

CHAPTER 12

CHALLENGE AND OPPORTUNITY

T WICE DURING SEPTEMBER 1975 Jimmy Draper was on the front page of the *Dallas Morning News*. Reporters speculated whether Criswell's heir apparent would jump ship. "Criswell Aide May Not Stand in Pulpit Here" one headline blared. Rumors then began circulating about the call to a church in Kansas. Before bedtime that day the Drapers fielded sixty-three phone calls at home from church members asking about the story and hoping it wasn't true.

Before his eyes Jimmy saw the prediction he made his last day in Del City coming to pass. It wasn't the way he had expected to leave Dallas, but he was both an optimist and a realist. He remained unshaken in his loyalty to the church and to Criswell while at the same time seeing that circumstances were making ministry for him impossible. The distractions became steadily more difficult. Once the rumor mill was in full swing and opponents solidified their platform for criticism, Draper saw he could not continue at Dallas. It wasn't his style to linger over such a situation but to be open to new opportunities to redirect his ministry. He preached in view of a call in Kansas, received a call, but said he "didn't feel the freedom to go." It wasn't of God. Further rumors then began circulating about a potential call to another church.

The next Sunday evening after Draper visited Kansas, he and Criswell met as they did before each service. Draper told him, "You need to say something to the people about all these rumors."

"Ah, Lad," Dr. Criswell answered, "I'll just tell them Dr. Draper needs his own church."

"Pastor, that's not true. You can tell them that, but it's not true. God called me to be your associate, and I'm happy to do that."

"Then you tell them what you think is best."

"OK, I will."

That Sunday night Jimmy stood in the pulpit before a capacity crowd with a live radio audience listening in. He wasn't looking to change churches and wanted to make sure people knew that, knew the truth. Plain-spoken and friendly as always, he shied away from any somber declaration of purpose and decided to make his point by a lighthearted reference to Mark Twain.

"You know," he began, "I've just gotten back from being away a week, and I sort of feel like Mark Twain when he read his obituary: 'Reports of my demise are greatly exaggerated.' I understand you are all here to hear my resignation. But I have no intention of resigning."

He meant it as a joke. The reaction from the audience proved that they took it seriously. The crowded sanctuary burst into applause, and the congregation rose to their feet as one. Some even cheered. Jimmy noticed that Betty Criswell didn't stand. Later he told Carol Ann, "If it wasn't over before, it's over now."

Looking back on that moment, Jimmy said, "I felt it was time for me to go somewhere else."

During those dark times God brought great friends into Jimmy's life. One of them was Paige Patterson, president of Criswell College, which was run by First Baptist Dallas. Jimmy had been instrumental in bringing Paige to Criswell College. Their fathers had been friends in the ministry a generation before, and Paige and Jimmy both began their ministries as teenage evangelists. Dr. Patterson saw the web of intrigue Mrs. Criswell was spinning in opposition to Brother Jimmy and went out of his way to defend his friend.

Patterson observed that Draper was deeply hurt by the breach of trust on Dr. Criswell's part, and did what he could to encourage the embattled associate pastor. "Someday," Patterson predicted, "you'll be president of the Convention."

"How do you know?" Draper asked, surprised.

"God always rewards people who do things His way. He will raise you up."

Another old friend, Luther Dyer, was a special blessing that storm-tossed summer of 1975. One night when the enormity of the situation hit him with full force, Jimmy sat at home at the kitchen table and cried, heartbroken. He called Luther, now living in Florida, and said, "I really need you here." Luther dropped everything, flew to Dallas, and spent three days and nights with him, talking, praying, and sharing his burden as a brother in Christ. Troubling as those months were, they were to Jimmy "special, special times."

Once it was clear Draper was leaving, he began getting contacts from several churches, taking them in turn and making sure each one knew about the others; he didn't want to run the risk of having two offers in play at once, lest it appear he was trying to bid up his services. First Baptist Church, Midland, Texas, wanted to interview Carol Ann and him, so the Drapers made a quick trip to West Texas for an interview. Another opportunity at Metropolitan Baptist Church in Wichita, Kansas, promised an appealing escape from an increasingly impossible situation. Yet another inquiry came from a smaller church in Euless, on the edge of the Dallas-Fort Worth metropolis.

Metropolitan approached Draper on the recommendation of the state executive director of Texas, Dr. James Landis, a college classmate of James Senior. They approached Jimmy based on his reputation without ever hearing him speak and launched a whirl-wind campaign to hire him. Three members of the pulpit com-mittee flew to Dallas on a private jet and invited Jimmy, Carol Ann, and the children to Wichita in view of a call. The Drapers arrived to a red carpet welcome. Each of the children was wel-comed to an activity, and Jimmy met with the office staff and leadership.

In a meeting with the deacons, Jimmy made a comment about the pulpit at Metropolitan, an elegant and commanding white marble construction that reminded Jimmy of the prow of a ship. Concluding that Jimmy didn't like it, one of the deacons present said, "Brother Jimmy, I brought that into the church. You just say the word, and I'll take it out." The pulpit committee explained that their offer to the Drapers included a car, the down payment on a house, and private schooling for the children. They loved Jimmy, appreciated him, and couldn't do enough to prove it. Rather than plotting against him, they were all pulling together to make him secure and content. "Everything about it was perfect," Draper commented, "except that it didn't feel right." When he sought that deep, final assurance from the Lord, it wasn't there. Draper couldn't explain it.

Jimmy and Carol Ann had visited the First Baptist Church of Euless, twenty miles or so northwest of downtown Dallas, when they met with the pulpit committee. As she watched her husband preaching at Metropolitan, twice she envisioned seeing him not in the marble pulpit there but at the simpler "Spurgeon's rail" pulpit in First Baptist Euless. Momentarily her thoughts transported her back to the more modest suburban feel of Euless, and the trendy orange carpet that would be so out of place in the sanctuary at Metropolitan. Carol Ann thought of how different the two churches were. Metropolitan made a prominent architectural and theological statement in Wichita; when she and Jimmy went to the church in Euless the first time, they couldn't even find it. They stopped at a 7-Eleven to ask directions, and the clerk there could not tell them where it was, even though it was only a few blocks away.

Back in Dallas Jimmy considered what to do next. He didn't feel God was calling him to Wichita, yet the church there was doing absolutely everything it could to make him feel welcome and comfortable. It was a dream situation. He stewed about the decision day after day, not knowing how he could say no to the Metropolitan pulpit committee after they had been so generous and accommodating. As he assessed the situation, "I didn't have the guts to say I couldn't take the job."

Finally one Saturday he gathered his resolve and called the church to decline their offer officially. He couldn't get anyone on the phone and, fearful he'd lose his resolve, sent them a telegram on the spot. The church was shocked and saddened that he would turn down so generous an offer.

"What did we do wrong?" the pulpit committee representative asked over the phone, genuinely astonished.

"You didn't do anything wrong," Jimmy countered. "You did everything exactly right. Nothing you could do would make your offer any more generous or appealing. All I can say is that it isn't the field God is calling me to."

The departing pastor at Euless, Bill Anderson, was a Baylor classmate of Jimmy's and recommended Draper for the position there, a recommendation affirmed by Roy Fish, a professor at Southwestern Seminary who was serving the church as interim pastor. The pulpit committee there asked Jimmy for a résumé. He didn't have one and had never in his life put one together.

He typed something up and sent it to them for their records. When they asked him to come it somehow felt right, though from the world's point of view it was completely counterintuitive. Dallas had an attendance of 6,000 a week, and Del City ran 2,300 when Jimmy left there. Euless by contrast had 900 people a week.

Draper preached in view of a call at Euless under the condition that the congregation would vote on him that morning. They did, he was called, and he went back to the church in Dallas to resign that night during his regular Sunday evening service. He had previously asked Dr. Criswell if he objected to Draper accepting a position in Euless since it was so close to Dallas. With a smile Criswell replied, "Ah, Lad, when you and I have done everything we can do, most of the people in Dallas-Fort Worth are going to hell. Go out and do a great work for God!"

He asked Dr. Criswell whether he should resign during the part of the service that was broadcast on the radio, or after they were off the air. "It doesn't matter. Do whatever you want," Criswell answered.

The service began and went along as usual until the time came for the sermon. Instead of turning the program over to Brother Jimmy, the minister of music continued to sing one song after another. In place of the normal ten or fifteen minutes of music, the singing went on for forty-five minutes. Criswell had told the music minister to fill the time, and not to tell Jimmy in advance what he was doing. Also before the service, Criswell had told the radio engineer than whenever Draper got up and walked toward the pulpit for the sermon, he was to cut off the live broadcast and play one of Criswell's old sermons on tape instead. The engineer did as he was told; Jimmy had no idea he was preaching into a dead radio mike. Since he and Criswell had agreed to always end the sermon with an invitation while the radio audience was listening, he preached a very brief message, and by his estimation, "One of the worst sermons I have ever preached!"

The slights continued. The next Sunday was the Drapers' last official day at First Baptist Dallas, an occasion for Jimmy formally to close out his ministry there and say his good-byes. Dr. Criswell had other plans. During that last week he queried Brother Jimmy: "Lad, do you really want to help me?"

"Of course I do, pastor."

"Then don't come to the worship services next Sunday morning."

Draper dutifully agreed, but when Carol Ann heard of Criswell's request she was deeply hurt. There was a disheveled protester who sometimes picketed on the sidewalk outside the church in a robe and slippers. Carol Ann said, only half joking, "I thought about picketing in my robe with a sign that said, 'I can't worship at the church of my choice today!' But we didn't want a fight. When a church fights, Satan always wins."

Grandmother Draper was equally incensed. "Mother never carried grudges," Brother Jimmy observed, "but I'm not sure she ever forgave Criswell for asking us not to come to worship that last Sunday morning."

On Jimmy's last Sunday night, at Criswell's direction, there was no sermon, only the Lord's Supper. Afterwards there was a farewell reception for the Drapers. A thousand people came. There was no room to sit or move around, and the refreshments ran out almost immediately.

In the aftermath of the experience Jimmy concluded that, yes, W. A. Criswell was naïve, but he played his naïveté to the hilt. He was crafty enough to let Betty Criswell and her sympathizers have free rein; he could argue he had no hand in events even as he admitted to Draper that Mrs. Criswell was jealous of him and hated him for his popularity. Draper was disappointed because people he trusted betrayed that trust. Yet despite what happened he never lost his respect for Dr. Criswell and Criswell's great work at Dallas.

"He was one of the most brilliant men I've ever been around and without a doubt the easiest man to love I have ever met," Jimmy mused, "but he refused, after avoiding it meticulously for thirty years, to get caught between factions in the church. I don't blame him for that. He was scrambling trying to protect the church." The scramble continued to some extent even after Jimmy was gone. Several members who had come to Christ under his ministry in Dallas requested that Jimmy come back to Dallas to perform their weddings. First Baptist Church Dallas had more than one hundred weddings each year, and visiting ministers were often invited to officiate. But after he had done several weddings, Charles Bristow, the facilities manager, called and said "somebody" at the church refused to allow it and that he was not to be allowed to do any more.

Carol Ann was especially thankful that the criticism of Jimmy's enemies never seemed to affect their children. "It was never a topic of conversation with our kids," she said. "My prayer every day was that the Lord would protect my children from being scarred by so-called Christian people. I believe we got through without any scars. Anger and regret only hurt us. I'm grateful that the Lord in His grace let us walk through. The people at Dallas heard Jimmy's message, and they saw his message in the way he lived his life and the way he responded to the attacks.

"I wouldn't take anything for the experience, but I wouldn't ask the Lord to do it again."

One close observer of events insisted Dr. Criswell was "heart-broken" over the circumstances of Jimmy's departure, but that despite his awe-inspiring public persona, he often yielded to the iron will of his wife.

The closest Criswell ever came to publicly acknowledging the truth of the matter was during a deacon's meeting several years later when he reportedly said, "I had a young man here one time, and I brought him in here to be my associate. I made the mistake of listening to the wrong people. It was the biggest mistake of my life. I should have never let him go."

Summing up those twenty-six tumultuous months in Dallas, Draper said recently, "Criswell was a great man whom I greatly admired for the rest of his life. I wouldn't take anything for the experience of serving under him.

"I was glad when I went there. And I was glad when I left."

Draper continued to communicate regularly with Criswell over the years. They often appeared on conference and convention programs together. Criswell would usually refer to Jimmy as "my young Timothy." They talked on the phone from time to time, and in the last visit they had together, God truly did a remarkable thing. Criswell was in the last months of his life. He was staying at that time in a hospital bed in the home of his close friend Jack Pogue. Jimmy had flown into town for a meeting in Dallas and came by to visit with Criswell.

O. S. Hawkins, former pastor at First Baptist Church Dallas and now president of the Southern Baptist Annuity Board, was there, along with Jack Pogue. At one point in the visit, Hawkins said, "Pastor, you know no one loves you any more than Jimmy Draper." To which Criswell responded, "Yes, and he has every reason to hate me."

Hawkins asked, "Pastor, why do you say that?" Criswell replied, "Because when he was with me, some people came against him, and I didn't stand with him." In a tearful and emotional time, they were able to rejoice in the faithfulness of God and in the purposes of God being fulfilled in each of their lives. It was a moment Draper would long remember and cherish as they prayed and wept together, and expressed the love they shared for the Lord and for each other.

CHAPTER 13

PREACHERS
AND POLITICS

JIMMY SOLD HIS HOUSE in the northern sector of Dallas and moved twenty miles southwest to Euless, halfway between Dallas and Fort Worth near the edge of DFW Airport. From a weekly attendance of six thousand he moved to nine hundred; from a pressure cooker atmosphere of suspicion and backbiting he moved to an environment where he was universally respected and appreciated.

Brother Jimmy retained his seats on the Annuity Board and the Baylor Board of Trustees. From the vantage point of the Baylor board he watched as the moderate/conservative conflict continued gathering steam. Along with many other Southern Baptist leaders, Draper believed most of his Baptist brethren were conservative at heart; it was only at the schools where, under the cloak of academic freedom, moderate professors nurtured nests of liberalism that questioned the accuracy and authority of the Bible.

A crisis similar to the one caused by *The Message of Genesis* developed when Broadman Press published the first volume of a new Bible commentary on Genesis in 1969. The publisher had infuriated moderates earlier in the year by publishing W. A. Criswell's *Why I Preach That the Bible Is Literally True,* a book that took a position of biblical inerrancy in opposition to *The Message of Genesis.* Criswell was elected president of the Southern Baptist Convention in New Orleans that summer, and the Broadman Bible Commentary, which leaned strongly in a moderate direction, was released the following October.

According to pastor and author Jerry Sutton, Criswell was "without a doubt the ideological godfather of the conservative movement." Whatever his private personal shortcomings, Criswell commanded the respect and attention of all Southern Baptists when he wrote in *Why I Preach . . . ,* "If we accept the teaching of Jesus Christ, we must accept the whole Bible, for Jesus Christ has set his stamp of authority upon the entire Book."

Looking back over the past eight or nine years, thinking particularly of the increasingly embattled and defensive seminary professors defending their freedom to seek the truth wherever the journey led them, Criswell declared:

> The divine origin of the Scriptures is now disputed in the name of scholarship, science, and religion. This is being done by those who profess to be friends and champions of the Word of God. Much of the learning and theological activity of the present hour is dedicated to the attempt to discredit and destroy the authenticity and authority of God's Word. The result of this is that thousands of nominal Christians are plunged into seas of doubt. Many of those who are paid to stand in our pulpits and defend the truth of God are now the very ones who are engaged in sowing the seeds of unbelief and destroying the faith of those to whom they minister.

The Broadman Commentary on Genesis gave its critics plenty of examples of seed-sowing. The writer, British Baptist G. Henton Davies, saw Genesis as a series of illustrative examples and psychological probings. For example, he commented on the story in Genesis 22 of Abraham and Isaac, Abraham's only legitimate son and a child of his old age. Abraham faithfully prepares to sacrifice Isaac at God's command; at the last minute his faith is honored and Isaac is spared.

Davies wrote: "Did God make, would God in fact have made, such a demand upon Abraham or anybody else except himself? Our answer . . . is no. Indeed, what Christian or humane conscience could regard such a command as coming from God?" The explanation for Abraham's action, according to Davies, was "Abraham's conviction that his son must be sacrificed is the climax of the psychology of life."

In 1970, the year Draper moved from Red Bridge to Del City, the Southern Baptist Convention approved a motion to order Broadman to scrap the Genesis commentary and write a new one "with due consideration of the conservative viewpoint." It was approved by the messengers in Denver that year by a margin of more than two to one. (The book was not withdrawn by the time of the next convention. Two years later a motion failed suggesting that the Sunday School Board pull the whole commentary series because it was "out of harmony with the spirit and letter of the Baptist Faith and Message.")

However, another motion aimed more squarely at seminary professors was not approved. It proposed that the Convention "obtain annually, as a condition of continued employment, a written statement . . . to be an affirmation of the individual employee's personal acceptance and belief in the Bible as the authoritative, authentic, inspired, infallible Word of God." The motion, and

Jimmy's parents,
James Thomas Draper Sr. and
Lois Jeanne Keeling Draper.

James T. Draper Jr.,
on August 3, 1937, a couple
of months shy of his second
birthday. Brother George
would come along in 1941,
Charlie in 1947.

Jimmy and his parents on
the day his father (holding
diploma) graduated from
Southwestern Seminary.
With them is Mrs. Frederick
Macomber, James Sr.'s foster
mother.

During World War II, Jimmy lived in Bay City, Texas, where he was baptized by his father at the First Baptist Church.

Armed with at least one squirt gun, Jimmy attends Piney Woods Encampment in East Texas. The family camped there during the summers, where in 1948 Jimmy felt God calling him to rededicate his life. Two years later he surrendered to preach.

YOUTH REVIVAL

Riverview Baptist Church

2709 Telephone Road

March 22 thru 29

~~~~

7:30 p.m. Daily

JAMES DRAPER
PREACHER

CHARLES SWINDOLL
SINGER

CHARLES OGLESBY
PREACHER

With friends Charles Swindoll and Charles Dan Oglesby, Jimmy held youth-led revivals in and around Houston before his graduation in 1953.

Sophomore year at Baylor, when Jimmy preached revivals on weekends and worked as a cafeteria busboy during the week.

In the pulpit at Union Hill Baptist Church, 1955.

By the time he graduated from Baylor in 1957, Jimmy was serving in his first pastorate and had been married almost a year to the former Carol Ann Floyd. Their first child, James Randall, was born in September.

Graduation from Southwestern Seminary, his father's alma mater, in 1961, with James Sr. (right) and seminary president Dr. Robert Naylor (center).

Jimmy and Carol Ann in San Antonio, 1964, with children Randy (7), Bailey (4), and Terri (3). As pastor of University Park Baptist Church, Jimmy oversaw an ambitious building program and organized support for a Hispanic mission congregation.

The Drapers in Del City, Oklahoma, early 1970s, the era when electric guitars came into their church and hippies moved into their house.

Jimmy designed the
pulpit at Del City in
the shape of a cross.

In the summer of 1973,
Jimmy became associate
pastor at First Baptist
Church, Dallas, one of
the largest and most
important congregations
in the denomination. His
Sunday night sermons
were broadcast on KRLD.

A staff meeting with the legendary pastor of First Baptist Dallas, W. A. Criswell. Many members expected Draper to take Criswell's place when he retired.

A big smile hid a host of challenges, the greatest of which was a faction at FBC Dallas that wanted Draper gone because it was convinced he was after Criswell's job. "I wouldn't take anything for the experience," Carol Ann said of their twenty-six tumultuous months in Dallas, "but I wouldn't ask the Lord to do it again."

Jimmy's friendships
with prominent public
figures have included
Billy Graham, Cliff
Barrows, and Dallas
Cowboys head coach
Tom Landry.

As president-elect
of the Southern
Baptist Convention,
Jimmy gives a
press conference in
New Orleans, 1982.
Winner in a four-
way race that year,
he was reelected
unopposed the
next year in
Pittsburgh.

Address to the SBC after his reelection as president, 1983. With the
moderate/conservative controversy at a fever pitch, he admonished,
"Our only hope for strength and vitality in our denomination is our
renewed and continued commitment to the Bible, this divinely inspired,
uniquely transmitted, carefully preserved, and totally reliable book."

Reception in Manhattan honoring Christian Ministries to the United Nations with Elias Golonka (left) and Ted Mall (right).

Preaching on world outreach at his alma mater, Southwestern Seminary, 1989.

Jimmy has made more than a dozen missionary visits to Africa beginning in 1986. Here he speaks with members of Oloirowua Baptist Church, 1989.

Street preaching in Africa with a local pastor/translator. Sometimes they drew a crowd with a bullhorn that played "The Eyes of Texas."

Ushindi Baptist Church, Mombassa, during the Kenya Coast Crusade, July 1990. Jimmy led a missionary team of 536 people from 16 states on a month-long trip, recording nearly 70,000 professions of faith. The last Sunday, Jimmy joined a dozen other pastors in baptizing more than 1,000 new Christians in the Indian Ocean.

Jimmy and Carol Ann enjoy a rare moment of leisure during a trip to South Africa.

Jimmy's first visit to Israel was in 1968, a Christmas gift to him and Carol Ann from their congregation at Red Bridge. Above, he meets on New Year's Day 1990 with the Israeli head of state, Prime Minister Yitshak Shamir. The same day, he presents the mayor of Jerusalem, Teddy Kollek, with a proclamation.

Jimmy with Ed Young (right), pastor of Second Baptist Church in Houston, and James Dobson for a Focus on the Family radio broadcast in 1993.

In 1995, at BWA in Buenos Aires, Argentina, from left are Richard Land, Sandy and Bailey Smith, Jimmy, Paige Patterson, and Carol Ann.

Billy and Ruth Graham, and Carol Ann and Jimmy at the Graham's home in North Carolina. The two couples have been friends in ministry for a generation.

Carol Ann and Jimmy with Franklin Graham, 1997.

After James Sr.'s death in 1966, Jimmy's mother, Lois, lived with him and Carol Ann as part of the family for more than thirty years.

The Draper Family in 1990 on their fifteenth anniversary at First Baptist Church, Euless, Texas. From left are Randy, Elizabeth, Kyle, Kevin, Jimmy and Carol Ann, Kim, Bailey, Wes, Terri, and Mike.

By 2000 LifeWay Christian Resources was flourishing under Jimmy Draper's management. After thirty-five years as a pastor, he had found new success as head of a $400-million-plus corporation.

another with similar wording pertaining to writers published by the Board, were ruled out of order.

At the close of that convention, one messenger spoke for many when he rose to congratulate Dr. Criswell on his leadership during these divisive times: "Without that man's sincere confidence in the Lord's presence in the life of the Southern Baptist Convention, his respect for fellow Baptists who disagree with him, and his tension-relieving, nonconventional but fair presiding, this Convention would have been complete pandemonium. In my humble opinion President Criswell has been God's man for Southern Baptist leadership in these crucial days."

W. A. Criswell was an unalloyed conservative and the most respected spokesman for the cause. What neither he nor any of the other staunchly conservative Convention presidents of the 1960s and 70s realized was that they themselves had the power to change things. There was no problem getting endorsements for conservative causes: biblical inerrancy was reaffirmed year after year. The problem was installing leaders who would carry out those conservative policies.

This was the problem tackled and solved by Judge Paul Pressler, a dedicated Houston layman whose family had been Texas Baptists for generations. Pressler met Paige Patterson in 1967 when Patterson was a student at New Orleans Theological Seminary. The two shared a concern for the future of Southern Baptists and a resolve to do something to halt the drift they saw away from inerrancy. They became a potent force in the conservative movement that gathered steam throughout the 1970s; Jerry Sutton characterized Pressler as the "organizer and strategist" of the movement and Patterson as the spokesman and "apologist."

The conservative movement achieved critical mass in 1975 after Pressler met William Powell, then leader of a group called the Baptist Faith and Message Fellowship. It was from Powell that Pressler learned how the bureaucracy of the Southern Baptist Convention turns on the Committee on Committees, which nominates members for the Committee on Nominations (then called the Committee on Boards). The Committee on Nominations subsequently generates lists of nominees for all the SBC boards, agencies, and commissions, including replacement members for the boards of all six Southern Baptist seminaries. Obviously, the theological viewpoint of the people nominated depends on who does the nominating. And the Committee on Committees, the fountainhead of the whole process, is *appointed* by the president of the Convention. According to convention by-laws, the appointments are made "in conference with the vice-presidents," with "in conference" being undefined.

It would take a while to effect any real change because terms of service on the various boards lasted as long as ten years including reelection options. But a conservative president who did his homework and appointed a reliably conservative Committee on Committees could start reclaiming the seminaries from the moderates. A decade of conservative presidents would complete the process.

As the conservative movement gathered steam, Judge Pressler explained this to Dr. Criswell several years after his two years as president. In his autobiography, *A Hill on Which to Die*, Pressler recalled the night in 1978 when he, Paige Patterson, and Jerry Vines met with Criswell:

> We explained very carefully how the SBC president appoints the Committee on Committees. . . . We talked about how a real impact could be made on our institutions through a continuation of conservative appointments.

After discussing this thoroughly, Dr. Criswell put his hands on the desk, pushed back, and looked at the three of us. His exact words still ring in my ears: "If I had only known what you explained to me tonight when I was president of the Convention, things could have been different.

". . . Do you know . . . how I made the appointment to the Committee on Committees? I received a call from Porter Routh (who was then executive secretary of the convention), and he said to me that I had to make the appointments in the near future. I said, 'Porter, I don't know who to appoint. How about your drawing up the list for me and letting me sign it?' And that's exactly what happened."

Criswell admonished Pressler and the others to encourage future conservative presidents to use their power to appoint "like-minded persons," and get to know conservative prospective appointees throughout the country. "His counsel proved a very valuable stimulus" to Pressler and the rest.

The late 1970s were a time of healing and refreshment for Jimmy Draper and his family. Brother Jimmy loved the church at Euless, which blossomed dramatically under his leadership just as his other pastorates had done. He also retained the high profile he had gained at Del City and Dallas. By the time Adrian Rogers was elected president of the SBC in 1979, Jimmy was recognized as one of the principal figures in the conservative resurgence.

Draper had been nominated for president of the Pastors Conference before the 1978 convention and lost in a close race to Homer Lindsay, Jr. The next year Draper won that office, and Adrian Rogers, running against well-organized moderate opposition, was voted SBC president on the first ballot. To Jimmy it was proof that there was a huge underserved conservative base in the convention. It reminded him of the truth of his dad's belief that the denomination exists to serve the churches. Gradually, Jimmy believed, his denomination had come to assume that the churches existed to serve it; here was a startling turn of events the SBC leadership would not soon forget.

It was in fact the conservative congregations that were the healthy ones, as his own churches over the past twenty years could attest. The conservative churches were the growing churches, the ones that were transforming their communities. The moderate churches with their liberal theology were the stagnant ones in the group.

Even after Rogers's election, the long-running conundrum about what exactly Southern Baptists officially stood for remained unsolved. On June 13, 1979, Wayne Dehoney, pastor of Walnut Street Baptist Church in Louisville and a former SBC president, rose to speak during the convention proceedings. He was, Jimmy thought, more theologically conservative than liberal, though Dehoney identified himself with the moderate wing.

He said in part:

"I have just come from the news conference with our new president, Dr. Adrian Rogers. . . . I want to read to you what his position and my position [are on] this particular phrase [from the Baptist Faith and Message declaration of 1925, reaffirmed 1963:] 'The Word of God, it has God for its author, salvation for its end and truth without any mixture of error for its matter.'

"My interpretation and his interpretation of what that means–'without error'–is that we understand this to mean that in the original autographs, God's revelation was perfect and without error, doctrinally, historically, scientifically and philosophically. . . . We believe the Bible and we believe God's revelation was perfect to us, and if there are glosses or...a textual problem of a word or two, it is human error in the translation that has come, but the original autographs were God's revelation. . . ."

The statement was heartily approved by the messengers. Jimmy Allen, the outgoing convention president, was still presiding at that session, and Draper motioned to him for a private word.

"Make sure the secretary gets Dehoney's comments into the official minutes," Draper suggested. "If you do that, it'll save us a lot of headaches down the line."

But the official report said only that Dehoney "spoke to his motion concerning reaffirmation of the section on the Scriptures in the 1963 Baptist Faith and Message Statement," then listed the names of the three others who spoke on the motion. "The motion was passed."

Judge Pressler noticed the same serious omission. When he asked Martin Bradley, the SBC registration secretary, and reporters for the Baptist Press why the speech affirming that the Baptist Faith and Message Statement upheld biblical inerrancy was left out, they said, according to Pressler, that "they felt it was not something of interest to Southern Baptists."

Had the full story been officially reported, Draper believed "it would have saved us twenty years of grief."

Brother Jimmy was even more embroiled in a related conservative/moderate standoff beginning in 1978 at Baylor, where by then he was chairman of the Academic Affairs Committee of the Board of Trustees. During a meeting of the committee, Baylor president Abner McCall and executive vice president Herb Reynolds, who eventually succeeded McCall as president, came in unannounced and asked if they could present a recommendation. The committee readily agreed.

At that point Draper didn't know that the chairman of the religion department, Ray Summers, had submitted his letter of retirement. McCall and Reynolds were there to tell the committee that, and to recommend Jack Flanders as the new chairman. Draper and Reynolds had spoken previously about what kind of person the position called for, and agreed that the school needed "the greatest, most prominent conservative theologian in the world we can get" for the job.

Jimmy did not know Jack Flanders well, though he knew who he was. Dr. Flanders had been a professor at Furman when he was called as pastor of First Baptist Church in Waco. Abner McCall was a member of Flanders's congregation, and Flanders had been a supportive friend and pastor when McCall's first wife died. Based on the recommendation by McCall and Reynolds, the committee approved Flanders, by then a professor in the religion department at Baylor, for the position and reported its action to the trustees.

Soon afterward Draper and Professor Flanders met in Dallas for lunch. Flanders brought two of his books, *The People of the Covenant,* an Old Testament history, and *Introduction to the Bible.* When Jimmy had a chance to scan through *The People of the Covenant* he was mortified by what he read. Flanders and his two coauthors, Robert W. Crapps and David A. Smith, denied or explained away virtually every miracle in the Bible, painting it as a purely human book subject to the same limitations as any other. "I read it, and it made me sick to my stomach," Draper later recalled. "It nauseated me."

His first comments to Flanders were far more circumspect. On September 9, 1979, each wrote the other a follow-up note after their introductory lunch. Jimmy's daughter, Terri, then a student at Baylor, dropped off some books her father had written in Dr. Flanders's office. He hoped he and Jimmy were already becoming friends:

"I couldn't tell you just how pleased I was to have the opportunity to meet and visit with you in Dallas," Flanders's handwritten note began. "I have the feeling it is the beginning of a friendship." He closed with, "I shall look forward to seeing you on a visit to Baylor and to discussing with you *P. of C.* or *Intro. to Bible.* May we both be able to share the love of Christ with the world with our preaching and teaching and writing."

Jimmy's note, also handwritten, began on a cordial tone but then steered toward a more serious note:

"The meal & fellowship on Sat. is greatly appreciated. Thank you for bringing me your books. I have read about 1/4 of *People of the Covenant.* I do want to talk with you & will call to set a time. Your book approaches the Bible with respect & reverence, but over & again states that it is man's record of his understanding & concept of God. I deeply believe that it is God's revelation to man & not man's revelation about God. At a time when all our Baptist schools are being carefully scrutinized, I am concerned to fully know what is being taught. I do feel a real responsibility as a trustee. Please pray for me as I do for you. . . ."

A month later, as Jimmy planned a trip to Baylor for homecoming, he wrote asking for another meeting with Flanders and further clarifying his position:

> Let me repeat what I deeply feel and what I believe
> is the feeling of Baptist people across this state. The
> position of *The People of the Covenant* is not in keeping
> with historic Baptist belief and teaching. I personally
> will not be satisfied until the book is removed from the
> curriculum and every effort is made by the teacher in

the classroom to present the full picture of the Bible in
its various academic approaches.

It was, Draper believed, "basically intellectually dishonest. . . .
It builds no faith in the historic Baptist position, and it ignores a
whole segment of excellent scholars who have given their lives to
pursuing the understanding of God's Word.

"Whatever the outcome of our discussions may be, unless
I have some assurance in my own heart that this approach will be
used in teaching and a book more in keeping with our position is
used, I will have to pursue the matter further."

Jimmy called a meeting with Dr. Flanders and the six or eight
members of the Baylor board who were pastors. When he walked
in the room he was surprised to see the Baylor legal counsel,
President McCall and Vice President Reynolds there. It wasn't any
threat, however; these were all friends and brothers in Christ who
were trying as diligently as he was to solve the problem.

"Jack, I wanted you to hear this from me and not somebody
else," Draper explained. "I read your book, I can't accept the
things you put in there, and I don't think it's in the best interests
of Baylor for you to be chairman of the religion department."

Jimmy had talked with each of the pastors individually before
the meeting. Each one promised to support Draper's position, but
not one of them spoke in support during the meeting.

Faculty members rallied around Flanders and his book, noting
it had been used as an Old Testament survey textbook at Baylor
for sixteen years and was also used at seventy-two other colleges,
twenty-four of them Southern Baptist. During its use at Baylor the
school had received only one complaint about its orthodoxy.
"Now apparently," they reported, "a number of other Texas
Baptists for the first time find the book in conflict with their ideas
of orthodoxy and demand that Baylor cease using the textbook."

The report concluded with the faculty describing the threat they saw: "These demands raise grave questions concerning the academic freedom of the faculty and students of Baylor University and concerning the cherished Baptist beliefs in the priesthood of every believer, involving competency of every believer, the absolute soul liberty of every believer, and the individual responsibility before God of every believer in matters of religion."

Jimmy organized another meeting, this one including the religion department faculty and board officers as well as pastors. "The pastors were behind me," Draper said later, "*way* behind me." The meeting droned on all morning without getting to the heart of the issue. When they reconvened after lunch, Jimmy asked to speak to the group. "Gentlemen, I'm the reason we're having this meeting. The reason is that I don't believe Jack Flanders ought to be chairman of the religion department based on what he's written. That's the issue and we need to talk about it." The meeting went ahead, but at the end of the day there was no consensus and no plan of action.

On October 26, 1979, the religion faculty sent a remarkable and no doubt welcome memorandum to the academic affairs committee asking them for advice. "We need your direction in the present dilemma over the choice of textbooks . . . [and] about the direction our Department should take in the future.

"We invite you to take a thorough look at our entire program of teaching, both undergraduate and graduate, and make the necessary suggestions that would help us to more nearly meet the guidelines of the Board of Trustees as representatives of Texas Baptists. We have every confidence in your concern for our teaching program and pledge to you our full cooperation."

Jimmy prepared a detailed analysis of Flanders's book, affirming, "Without any question in my mind, the theological position of the authors of this book and the posture of the book itself is in direct conflict with historic Southern Baptist teaching and with the Baptist Faith and Message statement that was reaffirmed in the Southern Baptist Convention in Houston, Texas, this year. Because of this I have some deep convictions about the book and about Dr. Jack Flanders."

First and most important, the book portrayed the Bible as "man's attempt to explain his concept of God rather than God's self-disclosure and revelation to man. Repeatedly the Bible is pictured as being solely of human origin."

In the opening pages of *The People of the Covenant*, Flanders and his coauthors wrote that "the literature of Israel began to take shape as men brought together materials of enduring theological value. As the collections were being made, the community of faith was gradually moving to the acceptance of this literature as the inspired 'word of Yahweh.' . . . As one or another of these collections came to be of particular importance to the worship life of a segment of the people of Israel it would be looked upon as authoritative and binding. In it, the people recognized the authentic voice of religious authority speaking to them. In other words, they regarded it as scripture."

Notwithstanding the fact that the faculty had asked for guidance, Herb Reynolds blasted Draper and his allies. In his newsletter column of January 28, 1980, Dr. Reynolds referred to "the organized fundamentalist movement among Southern Baptists which seeks to impose upon our teaching institutions, in particular, a strict doctrinal (and creedal) position of biblical inerrancy."

As he went on, he pushed every button he could reach: ". . . the power that they seek can be achieved only if all our Southern Baptist teachers believe the same way and teach their students to do likewise until everyone is properly indoctrinated.

. . . Then we would not each have to be responsible for reading and interpreting our Bibles for ourselves under the Holy Spirit. . . . It would all be conveniently laid out for us by the priestly group who believe that they are doing for us what God would do if He was just privy to all the facts."

On July 18, 1980, the trustees presented the report on the department of religion that the department had requested in October. It was a keen disappointment to Jimmy Draper.

Regarding faculty appointments, the board of trustees "encourage[d] the administration to use continued diligence and caution in securing professors who believe the divine inspiration of the whole Bible, and that the Bible is the infallible Word of God and truth without any mixture of error." They also declared, "The purpose of the Department of Religion at Baylor University is to teach the Bible as the Word of God. . . ."

But two pages over, in the section on textbooks, the report read, "In order to acquaint the students with the various inter-pretations of the Bible in the Old Testament survey course not less than three reference books shall be adopted by the professor in each course. These reference books may or may not at the dis-cretion of the professor include *The People of the Covenant.*"

For all the committee's endorsement of "divine inspiration," the book that considered the Bible just the opposite stayed in the classroom, and its coauthor, Jack Flanders, remained as chairman of the religion department.

When the time for action came there were men who stood with Jimmy Draper in principle, but none would go on record with him in opposing Flanders as chairman. His old friend Luther Dyer had warned him it would happen. As a board member at Midwestern Seminary when *The Message of Genesis* controversy was at its height, Dyer had taken a stand against Elliott without any help from other conservatives on the board. "You're going to go out on a limb and nobody's going to go with you," he counseled.

He was right. Jimmy was subtly but effectively shunned from the board. He became the butt of jokes; his children were teased. Jack Flanders threatened to sue him. When Terri graduated a few years later, Jimmy was still a trustee and also by that time president of the SBC. "They didn't even let me lead a silent prayer" during graduation, he wryly observed. "I became *persona non grata*."

More than twenty years later, he had never been invited back to campus. It was a sad, small moment in the history of Baylor that drove a permanent wedge between Draper and the alma mater he loved. Disappointing as it was, there was never any doubt in Brother Jimmy's mind that standing for the truth, even if he had to stand alone, was more important than preserving any relationship.

CHAPTER 14

DRAPER
FOR PRESIDENT

THE 1979 ANNUAL CONVENTION was a wake-up call for the moderates that the conservatives–the "inerrantists"–had given up trying to work within the denominational organizations and would seek to gain control of the leadership. Most moderates thought it was a short-lived movement that would pass. Many of them accused the conservatives of stacking the deck by busing loads of conservative voters to the meeting and otherwise stage-managing the election. Others pointed to W. A. Criswell's ringing declaration during the Pastors Conference that the assembled ministers were in Houston "to elect Adrian Rogers president." (Draper's comment on that remark: "You couldn't make him say it, and you couldn't keep him from saying it.")

Elected president of the Pastors Conference at the end of the 1979 session, Jimmy presided at the 1980 meeting in Saint Louis. He insisted that politics be cast aside in the interest of Christian friendship and pastoral harmony, and they were. It was a worshipful, inspiring two days preceding the Convention. To the conservatives' surprise, Adrian Rogers declined renomination for the customary second term. One reason he gave was strategic: if he served another year, a new president would be elected in 1981. That convention would be in Los Angeles, a long and expensive trip for messengers from the South and from smaller churches, who formed the conservative core. If a new president were elected in Saint Louis in 1980, then he could run as an incumbent in 1981 against the moderate challenger. The 1982 election, in New Orleans, would be in friendlier territory for the conservatives.

There was a groundswell of support for Draper to be nominated as Convention president. His conservative credentials were impeccable and his success as a pastor widely admired, particularly over the last decade at Del City, Dallas, and Euless. The Jack Flanders episode at Baylor had further raised his profile in the conservative camp (and in the gunsights of the moderates). A Draper candidacy would also fit the evolving pattern of one year's Pastors Conference president being next year's SBC presidential nominee.

Draper had no personal aspirations to be convention president; he could imagine himself as a candidate but not as one soliciting the job. A good friend of his saw it differently. Bailey Smith, now pastoring Draper's old church in Del City, Oklahoma, had asked his friend Jimmy to nominate him. Having promised to do so, Jimmy couldn't in good conscience allow his name in the hat as well. He declined to be nominated. As his brother Charlie observed, "If he had never been president he would never have lost any sleep over it."

Jimmy went to a strategy session in the hotel room of John Bisagno, pastor of First Baptist Houston and Draper's predecessor at Del City. Among the others present was Richard Jackson, pastor of North Phoenix Baptist Church, who insisted he could combine the moderate and conservative camps if he could get nominated. Someone in the room pointed out how warmly Bailey Smith had been received at the Pastors Conference Jimmy had just finished chairing. According to Paul Pressler, Jackson answered that his own position was so strong that a hotel porter could nominate him and he'd still be elected.

The next day Draper nominated Bailey Smith for president of the Convention. Jackson ended up third in a field of six, and Smith was elected with more than 51 percent of the votes despite not having nearly the name recognition of a national figure like Adrian Rogers or W. A. Criswell. To Judge Pressler, these results were a signal to the "establishment" that "conservative support was far deeper and far stronger than they had ever envisioned."

Jimmy turned his attention back to his church at Euless and to the evangelism that had been at the heart of his ministry from the beginning. Though identified with the conservatives, Draper never passed up a chance to reach out to all Southern Baptists and all believers with a message of reconciliation. A series of sermons he preached at Southwestern Seminary in the spring of 1980 well represented his position on biblical truth and the duty of Christians to respect and love one another even when they disagree.

His text for one sermon was 2 Chronicles 7:12: "The Lord appeared to Solomon by night and said unto him, I have heard thy prayer, have chosen this place to myself for a house of sacrifice. If I shut up heaven and there be no rain, or if I command the locusts to devour the land, or if I send pestilence among my people, if my people which are called by my name shall humble themselves and pray and seek my face, and turn from their wicked ways, then I will hear from heaven and will forgive their sin, and will heal their land" (KJV).

The first thing God told Solomon to do, Brother Jimmy pointed out, was be humble. Humility would go a long way toward closing the ever-widening breach between conservatives and moderates, because it would focus Christians on their own shortcomings instead of those of other people.

Humility, he said, is the initial condition of God's moving and God's power in our lives.

He continued:

> To humble ourselves means to face the truth about
> ourselves. It means to be honest with ourselves.
> To humble ourselves means that we admit that the
> problem is with us. We as preachers particularly have
> become experts at what's wrong with everybody else,
> and we're always preaching and pointing our fingers,
> and we're always coming to conclusions, and we're
> always speaking a piece of our minds and drawing very
> strong conclusions about things we know very little
> about.
>
> You know, meeting people and praying with them
> has ruined some of my greatest prejudices, it really has.
> The truth is, the problem is with me. I am my greatest
> foe. It is in my heart that the battlefield is the strongest.
> It is in my soul and in my spirit that the temptation is
> the greatest. . . . The greatest exercise that any of us
> could take would be to humble ourselves before God.

In a sermon titled, "An Open Door," Brother Jimmy said:

> The church is not an institution for the retention of
> the status quo. The church is not an institution that
> exists for its own enhancement or its own perpetuity.
> The church is an institution that is planted by God to
> be a witness to the saving gospel of the redemptive
> purposes of Almighty God through Jesus Christ. The
> challenge is for us to be used of God in those kinds of
> churches, and our blueprint is the Bible. We have a

word to proclaim from God. Only in the Bible do we have a gospel to preach, and we must have a commitment to the word of God. . . .

It's important for us to understand that evangelism and truth are inseparable. Biblical evangelism requires divine truth. Divine truth requires revelation in language. Revelation in language requires the deposit of an infallible scripture. As soon as confidence is weakened in the integrity of our source material, evangelism is weakened to a corresponding degree. Without an authoritative scripture, the gospel is like a movie without a sound track, leaving us bewildered and uncertain about the future, and about the nature of the message and our salvation. There is no evangelism where His truth is not declared. That is the task of the church.

Jimmy never passed up the chance to share the message of Christ, whether it was with a church member, a stranger on an airplane, or anyone else. In 1980 he and Carol Ann went with a mission group to Brazil. Jimmy preached, and he and Carol Ann both went door-to-door witnessing for Christ. Carol Ann had a portable record player with a recorded salvation message and a tract with her testimony translated into Portuguese. Using the record and sign language, she carried on "conversations" that she thought were miraculous for the impact they made despite the cultural and linguistic barriers. Through God all things were possible.

Jimmy witnessed to taxi drivers and people on the street. They seemed far more aware of their sin against God and open to considering the gospel than American listeners ever did. The Drapers went on to visit Brazil again twice over the next three years. Jimmy preached revivals, and the church in America helped their Brazilian friends buy land and build a building. (The grateful congregation named it the Jimmy Draper Building. It still stands today in the state of Minas Gerais.)

Jimmy also took to heart the Bible's instructions to Solomon in the event God should "shut up heaven and there be no rain." The summer of 1980 brought fourteen consecutive days of record-setting all-time high temperatures in Dallas. One day the high was 114°. The string was snapped on July 7, when the high reached only 103°, two degrees short of the all-time record for that date. The next day's *Fort Worth Star-Telegram* carried the headline, "Euless church may seek rain through prayer."

Water rationing was in effect in the city. The fire chief worried about low pressure for fighting fires, and there was no rain in sight. A page-one story read, "Prayers for rain were offered at many Fort Worth area churches this past weekend and the First Baptist Church of Euless . . . is seriously considering a mass rally to pray for rain and relief from the heat.

"The Rev. Jimmy Draper, pastor of the church, says he plans to organize an outdoor service to pray for rain if the heat wave has not ended by next week.

"'Historically, people have gone to prayer when a drought has reached epidemic proportions,'" Draper said, though the city hadn't reached that point yet. It was a natural step to take because it was what God said to do.

Meanwhile back at Baylor there was another hot situation in need of prayer, in the form of a fresh controversy stirring among members of the board. In January 1981 President Abner McCall announced his retirement effective May 31, only a few weeks before the SBC Convention in Los Angeles. The trustees voted to name him to the honorary position of chancellor and promote Herb Reynolds, executive vice president and chief operating officer, to the presidency. Then in May, the month he retired,

McCall announced his intention to challenge incumbent Bailey Smith for the SBC presidency.

From his vantage point at the center of the conservative/moderate conflict, Draper saw this as a bad move for Baylor, one that further reinforced the aura of liberalism surrounding his alma mater. On May 4, Jimmy wrote McCall a heartfelt letter describing his concern, which said in part: "Whether you realize it or not, you have basically identified yourself now with those who are on record in other places as having a very low view of Scripture. I regret this for you and for Baylor University. The sad thing is that Baylor really does not need the good will of Texas Baptists to survive. I view this as another step that will widen the breach that does exist in the minds of many concerning the faithfulness of Baylor to the historic Baptist faith."

McCall made his position clear in a response written two days later:

> . . . in the 1930s . . . Dr. J. Frank Norris was attacking Baylor University and our Baptist theological seminaries for being too liberal. When I became the chief administrative officer of Baylor in 1959 there was a conservative group which was criticizing Baylor and other Baptist colleges and seminaries as being too liberal. . . . Some of our denomination are still now criticizing Baylor and the other colleges and seminaries as being too liberal.
>
> Thus to my personal knowledge an ultraconservative segment of our denomination for almost half a century have continuously attacked our Baptist colleges and seminaries as being too liberal. I have come to the conclusion that the Baptist colleges and seminaries make convenient whipping boys and are always going

to be under attack by this segment of our denomination. Thus this criticism of Baylor will continue whether or not I am nominated for the presidency of the Southern Baptist Convention. . . .

My concern is not the beliefs about the Bible held by the Pressler-Patterson group but the attitude held by some of them that all who do not agree with them in all respects are infidels and heretics and should be excluded from all denominational committees and boards and should have no part in directing the denominational programs. . . . That there will be some [theological] differences is inevitable in a non-creedal denomination. . . .

McCall allowed his name to be placed in consideration "knowing full well that it would cause some to criticize me and Baylor and that the odds are against anyone who challenges an incumbent president."

His allies hoped otherwise. On paper at least, Abner McCall was as strong a threat to the reelection of conservative Bailey Smith as anyone could be. A life-long Texas Baptist, McCall was raised in a children's home in Fort Worth after his father died in the flu epidemic of 1918. He had been a Texas Supreme Court associate justice, an FBI agent, and a successful lawyer. He became associate professor of law in 1938; ten years later he was the youngest law school dean in Baylor history. In his twenty years as president of the university he built a strong reputation as good listener and defender of traditional morality, taking on *Playboy* magazine, retail liquor sales, and his own drama department for the profanity in Eugene O'Neil's plays. He was Adrian Rogers's SBC first vice president in 1979. A little framed sign hung on his office wall: "Thick Skin Is a Gift from God."

On the day of the vote in Los Angeles, McCall happened to walk into the auditorium at the same time as Judge Pressler. As Pressler later wrote, "I told him that I appreciated him and that I hoped he would not allow his name to be presented because it was obvious he would be defeated and would be embarrassed. Although I tried to express genuine affection for him, I felt he was very uncommunicative." In a two-way race, Bailey Smith defeated McCall on the first ballot 60 percent to 40 percent.

After the Convention, Smith, Patterson, Adrian Rogers, and some others, accompanied by their families, took a working vacation in Hawaii at a School of the Prophets Bible Conference hosted by Patterson and his wife, Dorothy. One hot topic of discussion during the trip, according to Patterson, was whom the conservatives would nominate for president the next year. McCall's defeat put the moderates on notice that the conservative resurgence wasn't something they could keep ignoring. The 1982 election would set conservative and strongly supported moderate candidates against each other toe to toe.

In writings over the next several months, Jimmy Draper's name came up; the more the group talked about him, the more they liked the idea of him as their candidate. They felt sure that Duke McCall, past president of Southern Seminary in Louisville (and no relation to Abner), would be the liberal choice. Patterson and the others thought Jimmy was the man with the best chance to carry the day against him. Characterizing Draper, Paul Pressler wrote, "He had led many people to a saving knowledge of Jesus Christ and had built great churches wherever he pastored. He was greatly beloved because of his faithfulness to the Lord and His Word, his gracious manner, and his excellent preaching."

Just before the 1982 Convention, Paige Patterson called Dr. Criswell to tell him they had decided to nominate

Jimmy Draper in 1982. Criswell said he didn't think his former associate could beat Duke McCall. As past president of New Orleans Seminary, McCall would garner lots of local support in the 1982 Convention, and as a retiree had plenty of time to campaign. Criswell didn't think Draper had a high enough profile in the denomination, telling Patterson, "Even *I* don't know where Euless is!"

More than seventeen thousand messengers came to vote at the 1982 SBC gathering compared with under twelve thousand the year before, a sign that both sides considered this another watershed vote; the candidate elected president would determine whether the conservative movement would be nipped in the bud or continue to develop. Of the four candidates nominated Draper came in first, but without the majority of votes cast to win. Duke McCall was second, and the two held a runoff. Conservatives were afraid that supporters of the other two men in the first round, Perry Sanders and John Sullivan, would throw their support to McCall, which would defeat Draper. To everyone's surprise, those votes were evenly split in the runoff. Draper had led after the first round with 46 percent to McCall's 35 percent. On the second ballot, with Sanders and Sullivan out, the vote was 57 percent for Draper and 43 percent for McCall.

Dr. Criswell hadn't made the trip from Dallas to New Orleans, partly no doubt because of his advancing age, but also in part, according to Patterson, because "he thought there was no way Jimmy could win." After the run-off results were announced, Patterson called Criswell and gave him the news.

There was a beat or two of absolute silence. Then Criswell replied, "It's like the parting of the Red Sea, Lad. It's a miracle."

CHAPTER 15

BLESSED ARE
THE PEACEMAKERS

T HE FIRST ORDER OF BUSINESS for SBC President James T. Draper, Jr., was to reach out to both sides of the conservative/moderate conflict. One of Draper's great advantages as a leader was his natural tendency to befriend everyone, including people he disagreed with. To Jimmy, being on opposite sides of a theological or denominational question shouldn't keep believers from accepting one another brothers and sisters in Christ. He never wavered or gave any ground regarding scriptural inerrancy, but he worked tirelessly as a pastor and denominational leader to be fair.

Brother Jimmy looked at the divide among Southern Baptists: on one side, those who upheld scriptural inerrancy; on the other, those who believed that the Bible was at least part allegory, metaphor, or myth. One view held that the irreducible minimum requirement for being Baptist included believing the Bible is the infallible Word of God; the other side insisted that any "truth test" for a Baptist was counter to the tradition of the priesthood of the believer and opposed anything that smacked of creedalism.

In one of his first speaking engagements after his election, Jimmy ventured into the halls of academia, some of which harbored the strongest and best-organized opposition remaining to conservative theology. During the fall of 1982 he preached to the students at Southwestern Seminary, where he graduated and would soon be elected to the board of trustees in 1984.

His reception there showed how much Draper was appreciated by Baptists of every theological persuasion. Truett Auditorium was packed, with students standing in the aisles and doorways and sitting on the floor. The Southwestern campus newsletter reported that Draper was "fast acquiring a reputation as a healer in the Southern Baptist Convention." The students gave him a standing ovation.

Throughout the controversy, Jimmy was more and more confident in his belief that it wasn't the seminary students who were fighting against traditional values; it was their professors, promoting their liberal theology in the name of academic freedom, diversity, and the familiar "priesthood of the believer" argument.

The view was reinforced by the reaction a fellow Baylor trustee and former student body president had to a trip members of the Baylor Baptist Student Union took to Washington, D. C., in March 1983. Texas Congressman Jack Fields received a request from Baylor for a U. S. flag. Learning Baylor students would be in Washington, Congressmen Fields asked to meet with them. He was told that the itinerary had already been set, but at the last minute he was "squeezed in."

He was appalled at the liberal slant of the questions the students asked him. In a letter to Herbert Reynolds, Fields declared, "I believe most of the questions were fostered by the liberal viewpoints of the speakers [in Washington] to whom the B. S. U. students were exposed."

There was Arthur Simon, executive director of Bread for the World, which Fields described as "a pacifist organization primarily concerned with reducing national defense spending and increasing social welfare/international aid spending;" Walter Fauntroy, a black liberal from the District of Columbia who backed a spending freeze on nuclear technology and, according to Fields, "has been a constant supporter of efforts to cut funding for important strategic systems"; and Senator Mark Hatfield who, Fields believed, promoted policies "which would lock the U. S. into a position of military inferiority."

Fields wrote, "It greatly concerns me, Dr. Reynolds, that only the views of these men were planned to be presented to the Baylor students and that they were not able to hear the 'other side' of the argument on such a crucial issue as national defense." Fields was concerned that the embedded liberalism at Baylor was not only distorting the students' view of Scripture, but their view of American politics as well.

As president of the SBC Jimmy Draper drew on the same characteristics that had made him successful over the years at building churches. He reached out to allies and opponents alike with letters, phone calls, and invitations to personal meetings and times of fellowship; he worked to build as much consensus as possible without compromising his position on the Bible. He made note too of an important group of Baptists whose hearts embraced the conservative view, but who wouldn't stand up and be counted publicly. To them it was more important to stand together as a denomination than to defend conservative beliefs that threatened denominational unity.

Jimmy wondered how his father would have felt about the issue. "My dad would have had a terrible time with this controversy," he mused. "It's a battle of conservative theology and liberal denominational politics. When the high-level leaders went out to preach on weekends, they sounded like sawdust evangelists. Yet within the political structure they held to the moderate track in order to preserve the unity of the denomination. I don't know how that's possible."

It seemed impossible even to articulate the problem without being assailed by the opposition. "If you don't name names, you're painting with too broad a brush. But if you do name names, it's character assassination."

Jimmy held meetings with moderates to find common ground to build on, looking for a way to put aside the conflict that started almost twenty years earlier with *The Message of Genesis* and shifted to a more intense state when Adrian Rogers became Convention president in 1979. It was an uphill battle. Whether they were still too angry to talk, or still thought the conservative surge was temporary and manageable, he made little headway.

Draper kept thinking the impasse could be broken if the two sides could find a way around their sharpest disagreements and build on the points they could agree on. At one point he secured agreement from his own conservative allies that if the moderates would go public with specific basic statements of belief, they would stop their denominational opposition. "We're not out for the power," Brother Jimmy reminded them, "we're out for the truth."

The moderates edged in the direction of a reconciliation, but in the end couldn't trust anyone on the conservative side and decided to wait out the inerrantist wave. According to one participant, they later decided that spurning Draper's offer was one of the worst strategic mistakes they ever made. Jimmy was more than willing to discuss the issues, but he wasn't willing to divide the truth.

One positive result of his efforts at reconciliation was that Draper was acknowledged as unbeatable in the Convention presidential voting of 1983 in Pittsburgh. The year before, Draper won a four-way contest in a runoff; this time he ran unopposed. It was a sign both of Draper's leadership and the growing power of the conservatives. This was the fifth straight year of conservative control since Judge Paul Pressler had developed his action plan for reclaiming the denomination using its own bureaucracy, the way a judo fighter uses his opponent's own weight to overpower him.

In the Convention address following his reelection, Jimmy ignored the chance to capitalize on his win by condemning the defeated moderates and spoke instead of those elusive, commonly held beliefs that brought all Southern Baptists together as brothers and sisters. Specifically, he spoke of the inerrancy of Scripture, but he avoided those words: though all sides claimed to believe more or less in inerrancy, they didn't agree on what "inerrancy" meant. There was no admonishment, only encouragement; no finger-wagging, only the offer of a hand in friendship and service:

> We have taken seriously the challenge of sacred
> Scripture to reproduce New Testament Christianity in
> our age through the power of the Holy Spirit. . . . Only
> people with such commitment can become God's
> change agents in a sin-cursed world. Weak convictions
> and shallow beliefs have never impacted the world. We
> have been used of God to impact the world because of
> our firm commitment to our beliefs. We shall continue to
> make an ever increasing impact as long as we hold con-
> sciously and firmly to these basic, foundational beliefs.

The basis of these beliefs is the Word of God. From
every section of our Southern Baptist Convention
recently . . . we have heard affirmations of our commitment to the Bible as the final authority for Southern
Baptists. In this conviction . . . we must stand united.
Our only hope for strength and vitality in our denomination is our renewed and continued commitment to
this divinely inspired, uniquely transmitted, carefully
preserved and totally reliable book.

Even as the peacemaker, Jimmy faced situations where he had
to stand firm. Having controlled the Convention bureaucracy
to achieve their own ends for so long, the moderates now had
a suggestion for Draper: share his appointment power with his
two vice presidents. Harold Bennett, president of the SBC
Executive Committee, set up a meeting at the Southern Baptist
Convention building that included Bill Sherman, pastor of
Woodmont Baptist Church in Nashville, Bill's brother Cecil, pastor of First Baptist Church, Asheville, North Carolina, and Bill
Self, an Atlanta pastor who ran against Adrian Rogers in 1979.

The Convention by-laws required the president to make his
appointments in consultation with the vice presidents, but there
were no teeth to the regulation; past presidents merely told their
VPs what they decided. These men wanted Draper to agree to
change the procedure so future presidents would be required
to share their appointment power with vice presidents.

At the meeting it was Jimmy against everybody else. Finally he
declared, "We're not going to change the rules." The pastors were
furious. It reminded Draper of the numerous informal meetings he
had held with seminary leaders in search of a forum for them to discuss their concerns. Sadly Draper concluded, "The liberalism was so
entrenched there was no way to get together."

Over the years Jimmy Draper had written several books, mostly on interpreting the Bible, though there were others–including one titled *Say Neighbor, Your House Is on Fire*–about evangelism and outreach. As his second year as SBC president headed toward its close, Jimmy began writing from his heart about the issue at the core of the crisis in the SBC: the authority of the Bible. Jimmy believed that every problem, every source of discord, every ruptured friendship in the denomination flowed from a disagreement about something Christians dare not disagree on. The Bible had to be the only source of all truth.

He spoke about it and preached about it. Now in book form he could lay out the whole discussion for supporters and detractors alike to analyze. He titled the work *Authority: The Critical Issue for Southern Baptists.* In framing the argument of the book the publisher announced that Draper "shows that the belief in the absolute authority of Scripture is at the very heart of doctrinal purity and strong evangelical outreach."

Here in one place Draper articulated the conservative point of view in detail. Turning the moderates' argument back on them, he insisted that he wasn't interested in controlling what the seminaries taught, only in assuring the conservative viewpoint was fairly represented. He and other like-minded Baptists weren't trying to impose their beliefs, only making sure their beliefs were heard and considered:

> We are still basically a solidly conservative people
> who are committed to the Bible as the totally reliable
> Word of God. We realize now that forces are at work
> among us which are contrary to that basic posture. We
> have not chosen to demand immediate termination of
> personnel from convention institutions, nor have we
> endeavored to dictate a "creed" to which all Southern

Baptists must ascribe. Although this has been the accusation, this is not in fact the case. What is the case is that we are demanding the right to be heard as contributing, cooperating, and loyal Southern Baptists. There is no "take-over agenda" by which certain people are being promoted to key positions with definite and specific instructions for actions on their part. Instead, there is an attempt to get representative people on the various boards and agencies of our Southern Baptist Convention so that the diversity of convictions, so publicized by some, may truly be represented in decisions and policies throughout our convention.

Some have accused conservatives of trying to destroy academic freedom and excellence. The implication being, of course, that to be a conservative Christian is to be ignorant and opposed to real education and free inquiry. Yet, the opposite is actually true. In many classrooms, for instance, the textbooks used and the position of the professor give no place at all for traditional biblical views. Evolution is taught as being biblical, and Creation often ridiculed. Higher critical assumptions such as the documentary hypothesis of the Pentateuch are often taught as the only proper approach, while the "old fashioned" conviction of Mosaic authorship is either totally ignored or ridiculed. This is the height of anti-intellectualism. Under the guise of free inquiry, such inquiry is actually discouraged. Many of us do not feel that we can remain silent while professors use tenure and academic freedom as licenses to intimidate students and to ridicule beliefs which they bring to the classroom from their own

churches. True inquiry would lead to the honest and
fair presentation of all material so that the student,
being adequately trained to discern all of the elements
in a given matter, can make his own judgments.

. . . If Southern Baptists are truly a diverse people,
then the solidly conservative aspects of that diversity
must have opportunity to be seen in our organization
at the points of real opportunity for input, instruction,
and decision making. . . .

He also addressed the complaint by moderates that conservative Baptists threatened the doctrine of the priesthood of the
believer:

They are using the term, priesthood of the believer,
to mean that an individual Baptist has the right to
believe anything he wants to believe, and that no other
Baptist has a right to say he is wrong, criticize him, or
in any way interfere with his beliefs or with his teaching of those beliefs in our Baptist institutions. That, of
course, is a complete distortion of the doctrine of the
priesthood of the believer. According to Scripture, the
doctrine of the priesthood of the believer teaches that
all believers in Jesus Christ have immediate, direct
access to the Father through Jesus Christ, the only
Mediator, and that we do not need any other man, or
any other being of any kind, to intercede for us. Those
who misuse this term are invoking a doctrine that
means a great deal in Baptist circles, making it apply to
something to which it does not apply. The priesthood
of the believer has nothing to do with the concept of
what a person may believe and teach and still be
regarded as a "good Baptist." Baptists must continue to

be people of the Book. Certainly each individual can go
to God for himself and interpret the Bible for himself,
but this cannot be a license to promote nonbiblical
views without restraint. . . .

No one in his right mind wants to exercise some
dictatorial authority over the legitimate bounds of interpretation. Bible-believing Christians have long differed
as to the exact nature of the millennium, for example.
Will Jesus Christ return before or after the Great
Tribulation? Does man consist of two parts or three?
Does man inherit his soul by natural generation, as he
does his body, or does God create it immediately? Is
God's elective purpose for man conditional or uncondi-
tional? And the list goes on. Most Christians would
agree that there is sufficient doubt about these matters
that extreme dogmatism is inappropriate. Certainly
these matters should not be allowed to become a barrier to fellowship and cooperative effort.

The present crisis, however, goes much deeper than
this. "Interpretation," in many instances, has become a
convenient cover for a denial of scriptural authority.

He also tackled the divisive issue of creedalism:

. . . We need to have a consensus among Southern
Baptists as to the irreducible minimum theology that a
person must subscribe to in order to be acceptable as a
professor at one of our schools, or as a worker, writer,
or policymaker in one of our agencies.

He went on to suggest four points: the hypostatic union: Jesus
was fully God and fully man; substitutionary atonement:
Jesus died on our behalf to pay for our sins; the literal bodily

resurrection, ascension, and return to earth of Jesus; and the doctrine of justification by God's grace through faith.

If a person wants to teach in a Southern Baptist institution or wants to write curriculum or have a policy-making role in one of our agencies, then it seems reasonable that he or she be asked to subscribe to these biblical parameters.

There might also be a few additional Southern Baptist distinctives for those who would assume teaching positions in our seminaries . . . baptism by immersion of believers, regenerate church membership, and eternal security. . . . Surely it is neither narrow nor doctrinaire to require that a professor in a Southern Baptist seminary accept baptism by immersion of believers only. I do not suggest that we have some who do not believe this, but only to illustrate that there are some Southern Baptist distinctives that we must not lose. As Southern Baptists we do have some distinctive understandings of New Testament teachings. Diversity does not mean giving these up.

Draper suggested a "blue ribbon panel" to draw up a set of parameters for discussion at an annual Convention. "Perhaps some other process would be more effective," he concluded. "But unless Southern Baptists continue to stand for something other than simply cooperation with a program, in some political or social sense, there is no question that Southern Baptists will go down the same road that once-great denominations have taken. It will not be long before we will be simply a shadow, a caricature of what we once were."

Jimmy invited Herschel Hobbs, then pastor emeritus of First Baptist Church in Oklahoma City, to write an introduction for the book. Hobbs was a respected and venerable figure deeply woven into the twentieth-century Baptist tradition—he and W. A. Criswell were lifelong friends who had been in each other's weddings.

At first Hobbs wanted to write his piece without reading the manuscript but agreed to read it at Jimmy's request. The introduction he produced was short, less than two pages. In it he pointed out that "due to human frailty, we do not all interpret the Bible alike," even Southern Baptists who were as a group "conservative theologically."

Hobbs wrote that into the interpretation battle, "claiming friendship with people on both sides of the present difference in doctrine," jumped Jimmy Draper, who "avowed, when he became president of the Convention, that he *belonged* to neither side." Continued Hobbs, "No man in my memory has worked harder than he has to bridge the difference. Drawing upon his widespread friendships, he has brought together people prominently identified with each side—if not to full agreement—at least to talk with one another. . . . While specific in his pronouncements, he allows for those differences which are inherent in our Baptist polity and practice."

Soon after the book came out, Hobbs was criticized for aligning himself with the conservatives. His introduction itself became news, and the *Baptist Standard* asked Hobbs to write an article about it. Hobbs wanted Draper's opinion on the article and read it to him over the phone.

"Well, what do you think?" Hobbs asked after he had finished.

"It sounds like you're trying to back out of recommending my book," Draper answered.

"Oh no, no," Hobbs insisted.

Draper told Hobbs of a speech Draper gave at Southern Seminary in Louisville not long after becoming SBC president. Seminary president Roy Honeycutt moderated a question session afterward that was so anti-conservative and abrasive it brought Carol Ann to tears as she sat listening to it.

One question from the group was, "What is a liberal? Define liberalism."

Jimmy answered, "I'd say a liberal is someone who denies any portion of Scripture."

"Give us an illustration."

"OK, in Joshua 3, the Bible says the Lord caused the Jordan River to stop so the children of Israel could walk across the riverbed and enter the Promised Land on dry ground. Anyone who denies that is a supernatural act would be a liberal."

Later, Jimmy added, a professor who attended the meeting told him, "If you had said anyone who denies the bodily resurrection of Jesus was a liberal, you'd have nailed 75 to 80 percent of the faculty."

"You and I both know it's true, Dr. Hobbs," Draper said as the phone call continued. "Why won't you stand up and say so?"

Hobbs's answer was, in a nutshell, both a statement of why the crisis continued and an example of how many venerable denominational heavyweights felt about opposing official SBC policy regardless of their personal views:

"Because it's not common knowledge."

CHAPTER 16

DEEPLY DIVIDED

I N THE PAST, Southern Baptist leaders on both sides of the divide had accused Draper of being too soft. Some said he was too easygoing, too much a reconciler. *Authority: The Critical Issue for Southern Baptists* proved him capable of articulating a strong defense for the conservative view and then resolutely defending it. Many agreed with him, but almost no one inside the SBC institutions would stand with him. The administrations at Southwestern and Baylor saw him as the adversary. The one thing he could be thankful for was that even his critics thought he was fair.

Roy Honeycutt, president of Southern Seminary, blasted the conservative position and insisted that "fundamentalists" were "seeking to hijack the Southern Baptist Convention." A Baptist Press report of August 29, 1984, led with Honeycutt's declaration of "holy war" on "unholy forces which, if left unchecked, will destroy essential qualities of both our convention and this seminary."

In spite of Draper's extended explanation in *Authority* that the conservatives were only looking for a fair and equal representation of their views, Honeycutt spoke for many academicians when he fumed that the conservatives "now propose fidelity to their particular and restrictive theory about biblical origin as a test of both faith and fellowship." Conservative efforts were "damaging local churches, risking the destruction of our denominational heritage and compromising our Christian witness to the world."

The priesthood of the believer was threatened. "History is replete with horror stories of political bosses, demagogues and tyrants. Some people in every age demand a king, saying 'Big Daddy' rather than 'Our Father.'"

During a speech marking the 125th anniversary of the seminary, Baptist Press reported that "Honeycutt charged the 'independent fundamentalists,' whom he said are in their sixth year of their announced ten-year plan to take over the agencies and institutions of the Southern Baptist Convention, 'are seeking to legalize life by eviscerating freedom from the gospel. [They] have more in common with Judaizers of ancient Galatia than with the apostle set free on the Damascus Road.

"'If you meet one of these Southern Baptist Judaizers,' Honeycutt said, 'tell him those of us who are free by the grace of God in Jesus Christ shall not submit again to slavery's yoke. For us there is no turning back to a limited legalism, no turning back.'"

The audience of students and faculty gave Honeycutt a standing ovation.

The attitude reflected a growing concern in the seminaries that maybe this conservative surge in the SBC wouldn't be temporary after all. The concern was heightened at the 1984 Convention in Kansas City when Charles Stanley, pastor of First Baptist Church of Atlanta, was elected president of the SBC. It had been bad enough in Pittsburgh the year before when Jimmy Draper, after being reelected unopposed, made Stanley chairman of the key Committee on Boards. Liberals opposed Stanley and had in fact even tried to keep him from the pulpit in Atlanta. Now he was in charge of the group that filled vacancies at the seminaries and organizations throughout the SBC.

In September of 1984, Jimmy met in Dallas with other conservative past presidents, Judge Pressler, Paige Patterson, W. A. Criswell, Southwestern president Russell Dilday, and other key players in the SBC conflict to try yet again to find a way for defusing the situation. A front-page article in the *Fort Worth Star-Telegram* reported Draper was a respected participant recognized for his honesty and openness, and revealed he was one of the chief instigators of the meeting:

> Draper, immediate past president of the Southern
> Baptist Convention and pastor of First Baptist Church
> of Euless, said he encouraged the Dallas meeting as a
> peacemaking effort.
>
> Although identified with fundamentalists, Draper
> received praise from moderates during his admini-
> stration for his attempts to soothe the tensions in the
> denomination.
>
> "Hopefully, we can have more dialogue in the
> future," Draper said. "Everybody has to be concerned
> about what's happening."
>
> . . . During his administration as SBC president,
> Draper held several meetings of rival factions as he
> sought to reduce tension.
>
> "I didn't think it was appropriate for me to [call
> these meetings] now [that I'm no longer president], but
> I had encouraged others to do it," he said.

Unfortunately the two sides came no closer to resolution as a result of their time together. According to Dilday they were in fact more polarized than before. The article quoted him saying,

"I think both sides would agree that we came away with our positions all the more resolute and fixed. It seems the lines are more clearly drawn than ever."

Dr. Dilday also announced to the press that "he and other moderates will definitely try to unseat fundamentalist SBC president Charles Stanley" at the 1985 convention in Dallas.

The newspaper identified Dilday as the SBC heavyweight "who has emerged as a spokesman for moderates." To some Southwestern trustees, including the newly appointed Jimmy Draper, such a partisan position was inconsistent with their position. At a trustee meeting in October 1984, a motion was made "to instruct Dilday to stay out of denominational politics," according to newspaper accounts. Jim Jones reported in the *Star-Telegram* that Ralph Pulley, a layman member of First Baptist Dallas, made the motion—which was eventually tabled—during an executive session of the board. [The fact that the motion was tabled was seen as a vote of confidence in Dilday.] In a later memo to the trustees, Pulley explained he had concerns about a fiery sermon Dilday delivered to the SBC convention characterizing the conservatives as "proud brokers of power."

After working so diligently during his two years in the presidency to find points of agreement, Draper was saddened by Dilday's repeated accusation that "fundamentalist forces are attempting to dominate the denomination and are a threat to the Baptist seminaries and colleges."

Jones reported that

> a trustee who asked not to be named told the *Fort Worth Star-Telegram* that James T. Draper, Jr., new seminary trustee who is immediate past president of the SBC, told fellow trustees he was deeply hurt by Dilday's accusations. Draper was seen as the candidate

of the fundamentalist faction when he won the presidency. He said he tried to be fair to all during his two years as president.

Draper said in an interview he is concerned about Dilday's role. "I think he's gotten into an area of controversy and polarization that we don't need. I'm not critical of his courage or right to speak out," said Draper, pastor of First Baptist, Euless, Tex., "I just regret the inclusion of his voice to be a polarizing factor. . . ."

Draper said he agreed Dilday had some responsibility to speak as a seminary leader but he would like Dilday's statements to be less divisive. "I'd like him to speak out and invite all the people to come to the Southern Baptist Convention in Dallas next year instead of saying 'these are bad guys and let's get rid of them.'"

The professors at Southwestern closed ranks behind their president. At a special faculty meeting on November 13, they approved a statement that:

We reaffirm our president, Russell H. Dilday, Jr. President Dilday has spoken out on the issues facing the Southern Baptist Convention. We feel that he has both the right and the responsibility as a denominational leader to make his voice heard. We feel that our president has pointed out real and serious dangers which threaten this seminary, as well as the entire work of the SBC. We share his concern and support his courageous stand.

Dilday continued his public rebuke of conservatives. He labeled premillennialism—belief that Christ will return to earth before the millennium–as heresy. In a *Southern Baptist Advocate* article, Jerry Vines, pastor of First Baptist Church in Jacksonville, Florida, and a conservative ally, challenged Dilday: "I have never made millennial views a test of fellowship. I know of no Southern Baptist who does. I readily allow my brethren the right to differ with me on interpretation, but please do not call my interpretation heresy."

Speaking to an audience in Georgia, Dilday accused the conservatives of wanting to turn all Southern Baptist seminary students into "clones of Dr. Criswell." He warned, "The issue is not theological conservatism versus liberalism, or the infallibility of the Bible, the issue is control of the Southern Baptist Convention."

Dilday continued, "Are we going to be a Convention committed to pressing toward theological conformity and creedalism, or are we going to be a convention that comes together to cooperate in doing missions and evangelism and winning our world to Jesus Christ?"

Once more, Jimmy Draper's insistence that the battle was over truth, not power, was lost in the rhetoric.

President Dilday crossed swords with his trustees again in the months leading up to the 1985 Dallas Convention when Charles Stanley was up for reelection and the moderates were bent on defeating him. On January 14 of that year he summoned Dr. Farrar Patterson, an associate professor of preaching, to his office and demanded his immediate resignation. Among other reasons, Dr. Dilday accused Patterson of falsely claiming that the faculty vote to affirm Dilday's position in the denominational crisis was not unanimous.

Some members of the board of trustees believed Dilday was punishing Farrar, a tenured professor who had taught sixteen years at Southewestern, for opposing Dilday's outspoken moderate views. After a protracted period of charges and countercharges, the board voted not to uphold Dilday's decision to fire Farrar. Though a nineteen-to-twelve majority sided with Dilday, the vote to approve dismissal had to be two-thirds. Draper was one of the dozen voting against Dilday's recommendation to fire Professor Patterson; even so, he told the *Star-Telegram* he still supported Dilday's administration.

On March 22, the same newspaper carried a two-column headline reading, "Leaders Say Dilday Faces Firing Attempt." The article noted that with each passing year, moderate trustees were rotating off the board and new conservatives were taking their places. Kenneth Chafin, a former chairman of the trustees, said, "I think the agenda of the fundamentalists is quite clear. They would like to remove Russell Dilday from the presidency of Southwestern Seminary." Dilday had no comment.

Draper, described in the article as "one of the convention presidents elected as a favorite of the fundamentalists," said for the record that he foresaw no effort to fire Dilday. "While he and I would disagree on some things, I would not personally seek to fire him." However, Draper added, "I think he has made a very big mistake by being partisan [in calling] for the defeat of Dr. Stanley."

(Dilday was eventually fired by his trustees, but not until after Jimmy Draper left the board. At least once before that time, Draper played a key role in preventing Dilday's dismissal because he thought it would hurt the conservative cause. He believed Dilday wanted to martyr himself to generate support for the moderates. Jimmy's position irritated some of the other trustees, but in historical hindsight, delaying the action strengthened the conservatives' position whereas firing such a high-profile critic then would have strengthened the opposition.)

On June 1, 1985, ten days before the opening session of the SBC in Dallas, the Associated Press carried a story headlined, "Feuding by Southern Baptists Intensifies," which illustrated how polarized the two sides had become. It reported that the moderates accused the conservatives of using theology as "a smokescreen for a political power grab."

The article continued:

> "The issue is control of the Southern Baptist Convention," said the Rev. Russell H. Dilday, Jr., president [of Southwestern Seminary], a conservative institution and largest seminary in America.
>
> He says a powerful "fundamentalist political machine" has used "suspicion, rumor, criticism, innuendoes, guilt by association and the entire demonic family of forced uniformity" in seeking control of the denomination. . . .
>
> "I don't know anybody in the Southern Baptist Convention who would not agree the Bible is the inspired, authoritative word of God. [However,] I shudder when I see a coterie of the orthodox watching to catch a brother in a statement that sounds heretical."

Herbert Reynolds, the report concluded, "says a group of fundamentalist students 'maintain surveillance' on campus, operating like the Soviet secret police, 'a religious KGB,' and report to fundamentalist leaders." (This referred to some Baylor students having secretly tape recorded classroom lectures to bolster their claim that teachers were challenging biblical inerrancy.)

These were the kinds of public statements conservative seminary trustees had tried to stop. The quotes also gave conservatives ammunition for one of their chief complaints: educators and administrators who drew salaries from the denomination then turned around and belittled its beliefs or attacked them head-on.

Draper made headlines of his own when he discussed the prospect of putting his church's contribution to the Cooperative Program—the denomination-wide general fund used to support seminaries, missionaries, communications, publishing, and other operations—in escrow until the crisis was past. He also opposed SBC institutions openly campaigning for Charles Stanley to be defeated in his reelection bid. Moderates immediately accused Draper of "holding the SBC hostage" for political gain and "blackmailing" the church.

Of the thousands of Southern Baptist congregations, First Baptist Euless was consistently in the top twenty in annual Cooperative Program giving. Any news that it might withhold its funds was alarming to both sides. In an essay published in state Baptist papers, Jimmy explained that he had no intention of permanently holding back any money. Nor did he intend to see partisanship weaken the denomination he had served all his life.

"In an unprecedented move," he wrote, "three seminary presidents and the president of the Foreign Mission Board have attacked an incumbent SBC president [Charles Stanley] and his church. They have called for a convention-wide campaign to deny him a customary second term."

And they have done it without an announced candidate! Imagine, men whose base of operation and whose personal salaries are derived from shared funds (i.e., Cooperative Program) engaging in a blatantly partisan campaign to simply oppose our president.

This has brought added tension and distress into our current situation. It is this unwise move on the part of these men that has threatened the very fabric of our cooperative efforts. I fear that we will see a pulling away from the Cooperative Program as a result.

When people do not have confidence in the institutions and agencies they support, they will soon cease to support them. In that atmosphere of concern, I shared that we must do something to require our leadership on both sides of this controversy to sit down as Christian statesmen and work through our problems to a solution. If we do not do that, we will see the death of this denomination. I believe the current situation is that critical.

My statement that we might consider "escrowing" Cooperative Program funds was *only* in the case that it would be *leverage* to arrive at such a solution. At no time did I suggest we would not give the funds. Indeed, we will continue our strong support. However, we must demand that responsible individuals act in a responsible way and lead us out of this denominational dilemma.

The article was vintage Draper: looking beyond the polarizing rhetoric of opposing forces to plea for discussion and resolution of the problem. He corrected the opposition's misstatements without criticizing them. He held out an olive branch without backing away from his position. He acted decisively as a leader based on what he believed was right, regardless of the consequences.

In an all-out effort to unseat Charles Stanley, the moderates threw their support behind a single candidate, Winfred Moore, a pastor in Amarillo, Texas, and president of the Baptist General Convention of Texas. Both sides had put out the word that Dallas would be a showdown on an unprecedented level. More than three times the number of messengers voted that year as voted when Charles Stanley won his first term in Kansas City. When the results were in, Winfred Moore got more votes than all candidates combined had received the year before, but he still lost. Charles Stanley was reelected by a bigger margin than he had won in 1984. That year he had garnered 52 percent of the vote in a three-way race; this time he won 55 percent against a single challenger.

Soon after the results were announced a former SBC president, Franklin Paschall, suggested forming a Peace Committee to try and come to some resolution to the conservative/moderate battle. It was precisely the "blue ribbon committee" Jimmy Draper had suggested in his book *Authority: The Critical Issue for Southern Baptists.* The committee was formed, but only hours later it was temporarily forgotten in a parliamentary scuffle that reminded messengers afresh of how deeply divided they were.

A motion was made by James Slatton to change the make-up of the Committee on Boards; instead of being appointed by the Committee on Committees, they would be chosen from presidents of state conventions and state Women's Missionary Union organizations. Again this was a transparent attempt to change longstanding rules that had kept the moderates in power in the past, because now those rules were being successfully used to advance the conservative cause.

Charles Stanley ruled the motion out of order, and the parliamentarian, Wayne Allen, agreed, ruling that a separate motion had to be made to replace each of the fifty-two committee members. Repeated calls of "point of order!" including one by a former SBC parliamentarian standing on the platform, went unrecognized by Stanley.

Slatton appealed the ruling from the chair. When a show of hands seemed too close to call, the issue was put to a ballot vote. It was the first time in convention history anyone could remember a challenge to the chair being put to a ballot vote.

The challenge was defeated, and Stanley's ruling upheld by a vote of 13,123 to 9,581, further inflaming the rhetoric on both sides. Sam Cathey, an evangelist from Oklahoma City, thought the Peace Committee took accommodation too far and had been formed "so that the liberals, not the moderates, can take control. For years I've been saying we've got to take off the kid gloves. People who don't believe in the Bible can be mean as all hell."

Cecil Sherman, pastor of Broadway Baptist in Fort Worth and a Baylor alumnus, told a reporter, "Tonight there was a lack of honesty from the chair in dealing with repeated calls for points of order, refusing to give everyone a chance to have their say." C. Welton Gaddy, then senior minister of Mercer University, said, "I think this is the most brazen, insensitive disregard for congregational polity and the denominational process that I've ever seen. [Stanley] looked straight at us and wouldn't recognize us."

One of Stanley's defenders said in response, "He's not obliged to recognize hecklers."

Judge Paul Pressler recalled the moment in *A Hill on Which to Die*:

> The 1985 meeting in Dallas was, in many ways, the culmination of the convention controversy. The conservatives won decisively against all the liberals could muster. The liberals would continue to oppose the new direction of the convention, but after Dallas, many of them began to realize the futility of their cause. The people in the pews did not support their position, and now, with the new trustees elected in Dallas, the ability of the agency heads to lead the liberal cause was being curtailed. It was the pivotal event in the history of the SBC and a defeat from which the liberals would and could never recover.

CHAPTER 17

TEXAS REFUGE

THROUGHOUT JIMMY DRAPER'S TURBULENT years as president of the SBC and the controversies at Baylor and Southwestern Seminary, the First Baptist Church in Euless remained a nurturing and supportive refuge for him both personally and professionally.

The congregation's appreciation for Brother Jimmy began even before he ever preached at Euless. Some members listened to him Sunday nights on the radio from First Baptist, Dallas, and were attracted to his combination of friendly informality and solid scriptural grounding. When their previous pastor, Bill Anderson, announced his resignation to accept a call in Florida in the summer of 1975, the members moved quickly to elect a search committee and find a new leader.

As Jimmy would say later, the timing was right for him to make a move away from a pressure cooker situation. He certainly didn't have any plans to move to Euless, and there were other opportunities that seemed more attractive on the surface, particularly the one in Wichita, Kansas. But he felt God's guidance in a very specific way. On October 26, scarcely two months after

Anderson's departure, Brother Jimmy preached in view of a call with the understanding that the congregation would vote on him the same day. Out of 979 secret ballots, 967 were marked "Yes." Four weeks later, the Sunday before Thanksgiving, Jimmy began his new ministry and a new phase in his life.

W. A. Criswell had joked that even he didn't know where Euless was. Through the mid-1960s it was a small town of under five thousand on the prairie between Dallas and Fort Worth. But with the construction of DFW Regional Airport in the late 1960s, the population increased fivefold, and Euless became part of the dramatic urbanization that transformed the region. The congregation of First Baptist Church wanted to be a spiritual light to this vibrant community, and Jimmy Draper was eager to lead them.

Brother Jimmy brought an enthusiasm to the pulpit that infused the church with a sense of new opportunity and responsibility. In January 1976, only two months after he answered the call in Euless, the church oversubscribed its largest-ever annual budget of more than half a million dollars. Jimmy's preaching style was a reflection of that passion and commitment. He liked to move around while he preached, and wore a lapel microphone on Sunday morning so he wouldn't have to stand still in front of the pulpit mike. He also had the "Spurgeon's rail" pulpit, which had a semicircular railing around it, removed and replaced with a less-confining and simpler one he designed himself. From the front it looked like an oak cross, with the horizontal bar formed by the edge of the desk surface and the vertical bar forming the supporting upright. A little brass plate on the desk where only the speaker could see it reminded him, "Sir, we would see Jesus."

Observers called him "restless" in the pulpit, constantly moving, gesturing, and even walking around. Jimmy didn't read his sermons but preached a tightly structured message from notes.

Most of his commentary was based directly on the Bible—explanations of what the Bible said and why it was important. He preached through entire Bible books over a series of weeks, sometimes gathering enough information and insight in the process to write a book of his own. *Hebrews: The Life that Pleases God, Proverbs: The Secret of Beautiful Living, Jonah: Living in Rebellion,* and other titles were published during the Euless years; some had companion workbooks as well.

Brother Jimmy was a one-man whirlwind out of the pulpit too. As Ruth Eyre wrote in the *Dallas Times Herald*: "Every Monday morning he sends handwritten notes to 25 to 40 people, including every visitor who attended Sunday services at his church. On Saturdays, he calls on most of the Sunday visitors in person." If he was the first one in the office on a weekday morning, he put the coffee on to brew. If trash cans needed emptying, he did it himself without hesitation. There was no trace of pridefulness in him, and no task was too humble if it served the Lord and the church.

Jimmy instituted a series of new programs as the church and the community grew, and revisited some popular programs from the past. Wednesday night suppers, discontinued years before, were revived, as were weekly Bible studies for women. A 24-hour intercessory prayer ministry began in a specially reserved room. Volunteers served around the clock in one-hour shifts, praying over requests submitted on slips of paper. Various programs for both youth and seniors (dubbed "Keenagers") expanded dramatically as well.

Brother Jimmy oversaw the hiring of Euless's first director of evangelism and also made other additions to the staff. Some of the new faces were from churches Jimmy knew well. The evangelism director, Rick Braswell, was from First Southern Baptist Church, Del City, Oklahoma; youth pastor Tony Dyer was from Red

Bridge Baptist Church in Kansas City; and the new minister of childhood education, Bob Bachman, was formerly at First Baptist Church, Raytown, Missouri.

These men were all hired during Brother Jimmy's first year in Euless as the church scrambled to keep up with the growing community. Sunday school attendance was increased 9 percent a year and 130 or more visitors on average attended each week. Membership during Jimmy's first three years climbed from about 2,300 to more than 3,200; in time more than half the church members lived outside Euless.

To ease overcrowding the youth began meeting in the high school across the street. Though the church had built a new auditorium shortly before Jimmy's arrival, it was clear that they were again out of room. By the fall of 1978 the church had agreed to buy thirteen acres adjacent to their existing property and began building two new three-story buildings. A one-day fund-raising drive produced cash and pledges of more than $146,000.

However, the promising forward momentum was soon stopped by a dramatic rise in interest rates and a corresponding cooling of the market for construction bonds. No investor wanted to lock in a return of 8.5 percent when the rate of inflation was spiking to over 20 percent. Jimmy and a few deacons signed personal notes totaling more than $67,000 so the church wouldn't default on its construction loans. Eventually the bonds were redeemed for new ones issued at higher interest rates, and the immediate crisis was solved. Everyone involved agreed that the financial emergency had brought them closer together as a congregation, and more confident in their faith.

The first of the two new buildings was soon finished, but the second remained a fenced-in hole in the ground–"the swimming pool"–for more than two years before it was finally completed on a pay-as-you-go schedule in 1984. The only way to finish them sooner was to divert money from missions or other ministries, and no one wanted to do that: better to own a hole in the ground than to compromise the preaching and propagation of the Word.

Along with the challenges of the Euless years, Brother Jimmy enjoyed rich personal blessings. In 1977 his son Randy was married to Elizabeth Crossley of Dallas; three years later son Bailey married Kim Moore of Euless. In 1983 his daughter Terri received her degree from Baylor and was married the following spring to Michael Don Wilkinson.

One memento that Brother Jimmy cherished was a letter Terri wrote him when she was a junior in high school. At an age when many teenagers are in conflict with their parents, Terri expressed her appreciation for her father in a remarkable way. The letter said in part:

> You are my dearest friend. My respect for you grows
> deeper with every passing day. You have shown me
> that my happiness cannot be dependent upon things
> on earth, but must lie totally upon the Lord. You have
> never tried to push anything on me or make me some-
> one I am not, and I thank you for that.
>
> Your life has been witness to the fact that when you
> lose your life for Christ's sake, then you really live.
> Thank you, Dad, for being an instrument for the Lord
> to show me how much I need Him.

In 1981 Jimmy and Carol Ann celebrated their silver wedding anniversary with a trip to Hawaii. Their love for each other was stronger than ever, as Jimmy affirmed in a column he wrote for the church newsletter before her birthday one year:

> She has the grace of God upon her countenance.
> Her appearance is always beautiful and glowing with

His Presence. She has the capacity to always look like she has been preparing all day to be seen, even when she has two minutes' notice that I want her to make a hospital call or visit with me. We have never had an argument . . . she just will not argue with me!

Her glowing smile makes preaching an extra delight for me as she sits there at the front to pray for me and claim God's presence in that moment. Her sound counsel has never failed to be correct. She has always reminded me that God used me . . . but never because of my talent, but because of His Spirit. God has used her to challenge me in my Christian pilgrimage. She is so far ahead of me that my goal every day is to let God move in my life as He does in hers.

His compassion for others gave Brother Jimmy a gift for applying biblical discipline in a way that was redemptive, not judgmental. Many members at Euless had never seen public church discipline invoked until Jimmy did so. Preachers and members alike are prone to shrink from the hard demands of the faith, but Jimmy resolutely proceeded according to the Scriptures. Private sins remain private, but the biblical example shows that public sins must be rebuked publicly. Jimmy counseled his wayward member in private, gave him a public forum to answer the charges and repent, and Christian fellowship was restored. No one ever spoke about it again.

The church in Euless grew to have a deep attachment to Brother Jimmy and Carol Ann. When they came home from the Southern Baptist Convention in 1982 after Draper's election as president, church members met them at the airport, together with the mayor of Euless and the city council, and, as Jimmy described it, they were "whisked off to the church in a big black limousine with police escort." The first Sunday they were back, they were introduced in church as the president and first lady of the Southern Baptist Convention.

The official church history later chronicled Jimmy's triumphs as convention president, and the Tennessee state Baptist paper declaring the Convention in Pittsburgh during Jimmy's second term to be "the best Convention in recent years. It would be difficult to overestimate the contribution made by Jimmy Draper to the successful convention. The openness and honesty which characterized his year as president carried over into the convention session."

During his two years as president, Draper logged more than 300,000 miles, including three trips to the White House, speaking to the Southern Baptist Directors of Evangelism in Puerto Rico, addressing the European Baptist Convention in Germany, visiting national leaders and missionaries in Africa, and leading a group to Israel to meet Prime Minister Menachem Begin. Busy as he was, he worked continuously to heal the continuing breach among Southern Baptists and never neglected his duties at Euless, where both attendance and budget posted strong gains during his two years in office. By 1985, Jimmy's tenth year as pastor, the annual budget had grown from just over $500,000 to more than $4,500,000.

Even while traveling the world, Brother Jimmy kept sight of the needs of his own church and community. Since the church was near the Interstate, many strangers stopped to ask for money or food. The church met this need by opening a food closet. Jimmy's office door was always open to everybody from giggling Vacation Bible School students to insistent adult visitors with hard questions about Christianity on their hearts.

As one season and one year followed the next, Jimmy and Carol Ann embraced their church in Euless, worked tirelessly to build it up, dedicated themselves to reaching the world for Christ, and put down deep roots in the community.

CHAPTER 18

REACHING OUT

BY THE TIME OF Charles Stanley's reelection in Dallas, Jimmy Draper had stepped gratefully out of the national spotlight and renewed his work at First Baptist Euless with fresh enthusiasm. During his two terms as SBC president, Jimmy was on the road three to four days a week as a goodwill ambassador of the Convention. The deacons at Euless had approved his frequent absences at the start of his presidency, allowing Jimmy to represent Southern Baptists in the pulpit, on the mission field, and in other arenas around the world. In his capacity as president he attended everything from meetings at the White House to more revivals in Brazil.

As busy as he was, neither his congregation, his family, nor his neighborhood was neglected. "You determine what you've got to get done," he said. "If it's a priority, you'll do it." Whenever he was in town, Jimmy carried on the tradition his father established of visiting people at home on Saturdays, sharing the gospel and inviting them to church. He ventured into rich and poor areas alike, treating everyone as equals in the sight of God.

No doubt there were many encounters like the one Brother Jimmy had with young Todd Smith. Todd's parents divorced when he was five, and Todd lived with his mother and their poodle, Pierre, in a modest two-bedroom apartment next door to the church. Todd was amazed that a preacher as busy as Brother Jimmy must be would come to see them and spend so much time with them. It was clear to Todd that Jimmy treated everyone the same.

In church on Sunday, the youth sat all together on the right side of the sanctuary. Jimmy always made a point of looking at them and including them as he spoke. Todd thought Brother Jimmy communicated to and inspired people of all ages. Through the pastor's teaching and encouragement, Todd dreamed of accomplishing things he could never before have imagined doing.

In a step of faith, Todd ran for senior class president at his high school, even though he had never been in student government. He won, defeating the incumbent junior running for reelection, went on to study political science as an undergraduate, then enrolled in law school. While he was studying law, Brother Draper was president of the SBC. That didn't keep Jimmy from continuing as Todd's faithful pen pal and advisor. Draper answered his letters, sent him tapes to listen to, and continued to encourage him beyond anything Todd could have imagined. When the two were in Washington at the same time, Draper carved out an evening to visit with Todd, and ended up talking in his hotel room until 3 a.m. Draper not only told him, but showed him, what it's like to be a Christian.

Todd became a successful attorney and a member of the Texas state legislature. He credits Brother Jimmy as a major factor in his success. And there are doubtless many, many other Todds who point to Jimmy Draper as a great inspiration and example in their lives.

Terry Horton, who became one of Jimmy's close friends and later accompanied him to Africa several times, first became acquainted with him over some pointed theological questions. Terry moved to Euless from Arkansas and visited First Baptist Church but couldn't imagine going there; it looked like there were more people in the sanctuary than lived in the whole town he came from.

Horton had no idea that Brother Jimmy was president of the Southern Baptist Convention, but he wanted to know what this preacher thought about inerrancy, hypostatic union, the virgin birth, and other foundational issues. So one weekday he walked through Jimmy's open office door, introduced himself, and started asking questions. The pastor's open, friendly, Bible-based answers reassured Terry that FBC Euless was the place for his family.

Growing up a preacher's son, Jimmy was ever mindful of the toll a minister's life takes on his family. True, he worked hard and traveled long, but when Jimmy was home, he was home. His wife and children enjoyed his undivided attention when he was in the house; he was as passionate about being a husband and father as he was about being a minister. That meant that when he did have to be away, his family didn't resent the time. They knew he would be back, and as long as he was home, he was all theirs.

It was about this time that Jimmy's son Bailey got interested in bow hunting for deer. A church member took him on his first hunt, and he fell in love with it. Later he learned to hunt with a rifle too. Seeing his son's interest, Jimmy took up the sport as a way to spend time with his son. Within a few years they established a tradition of deer hunting every year the first week in November. More than twenty-five Novembers later they had never missed a season.

Despite the pressures and responsibilities of his work, Jimmy presided over a low-stress household. Everyone was encouraged to be himself. The children weren't forced into some mold based on the ideal of what a perfect preacher's kid should be. Jimmy said, "My sons are going to get in fights and kiss girls like every other boy." When Randy grew long hair and started playing in a rock band, Jimmy and Carol Ann gave him the freedom to be himself. And to a pulpit committee once, who asked how his wife would be assisting with his ministry, he said, "My wife is my wife and the mother to our children. She isn't an associate pastor." They shouldn't assume she would always be available to run a volunteer group, teach a class, or play the piano. They were not a two-for-the-price-of-one team; they were a family.

The Draper house was full of laughter and light-heartedness. A visitor one weekday afternoon might see Brother Jimmy doing chores around the house in a pair of bright orange gym shorts and a floppy hat, children and their friends coming and going, the inevitable stray house guest or two, and Jimmy's mother, who had long since become a permanent fixture in the household, busy in the kitchen. Jimmy and Carol Ann loved having their children grow up with a grandmother in the house. The Drapers' friends thought of Grandmother as an integral part of the family. She was included in all the family events and posed with everyone else for the annual Draper Christmas card photo.

Jimmy's two brothers were both in town as well, and the three families lived in the same place for the first time in decades. George, the middle brother, taught school for a couple of years in the 1960s before deciding to attend seminary. Then he left seminary after two years of study to begin his pastorate, serving in North Dakota and Montana before heart trouble forced him to give up his career. He and his wife, Beverly, and their adopted daughters, Rebecca and Elizabeth, moved to Euless in 1982, one year after youngest brother Charlie had settled in town with his wife, Retta, and their children, Shelly and David.

Charlie had been pastoring a church in Florida and felt called away from the ministry for a season. He returned to the pastorate in 1988 serving a congregation in Honolulu, and went on to become a professor at Boyce College of Southern Seminary in Louisville. George died in 1989 at age forty-seven following his fifth heart attack. Jimmy had met George's wife when she played the piano at his church in Tyler as a teenager. She said then that she wanted Brother Jimmy to conduct her wedding; at that point she didn't even know he had a brother named George. Years later Beverly and George both attended East Texas Baptist College in Marshall, and Jimmy wrote letters introducing them to each other. Sure enough, Brother Jimmy conducted her wedding–to his brother.

Along with their younger brother, Charlie, Jimmy also conducted George's funeral, and kept in close contact with Beverly and the girls. True to form, Jimmy promised Rebecca and Elizabeth, "I can't be your dad, and I won't even try. But I'll be the best stand-in dad I can be."

Like all the other churches Jimmy Draper pastored, First Baptist Euless was soon bursting at the seams and built a new building. By the mid-1980s attendance was 2,500 a week and climbing, with an average of almost three hundred baptisms a year. Eager to expose everyone in the church to the thrill of missionary outreach, he organized a Mid-Cities Mission Trip, canvassing neighborhoods around Euless, between Dallas and Fort Worth, witnessing and inviting people to church. It gave any member who wanted it the chance to participate in missions with "no shots and no plane tickets." The ministry, focusing mainly on area apartment buildings, eventually claimed two thousand people in Bible study every week.

The year after retiring from the SBC presidency, Draper led his congregation in forming a Crisis Pregnancy Center, where trained counselors met with an average of 350 girls a month to promote alternatives to abortion, provide counseling, and give medical tests. By 1987 First Baptist Euless also supported three mission churches and gave $700,000 to special missions offerings in addition to their Cooperative Program contribution of 11 percent of undesignated income.

In 1987 Draper was one of six Southwestern graduates honored as Distinguished Alumni. The conservative/moderate battle had abated somewhat by that time. Even so, during his remarks at the celebratory luncheon on June 17, Southwestern president Russell Dilday couldn't resist once again defending his faculty from people he considered conservative rabble rousers.

The next week Jimmy, ever the peacemaker, wrote to Dilday:

> It is time for us to lay aside and forget the few negative encounters we have had and pass along to the faculty the thousands of supportive letters, comments, phone calls, and other expressions of appreciation. We are creating a siege mentality in the lives of those faculty members and they live in fear of dismissal, reprisal and intimidation. We must not allow that mentality to continue any longer.
>
> . . . Anyone who is in the public arena will get criticism. I have a group in this area praying that I will be saved! However, I know my heart and I know that God has called me so I do not get distressed over that kind of thing, nor do I dwell on it.

Denominational discord remained a challenge to Jimmy and other Baptist leaders. At the 1988 convention in San Antonio after the conservative candidate, Jerry Vines, won with a scant 51.5 percent majority, a group of furious moderate messengers walked from the convention center to the Alamo, where they burned their ballots in protest.

Adrian Rogers sent Jimmy a copy of a letter one of his church members received from Baylor president Herbert Reynolds just after the Convention, which warned of "the desire by the Fundamentalists to create a priestly order among Baptists and to have us become a creedal, hierarchical denomination. If the Fundamentalists are not stopped we will become more and more like the Roman Catholic Church. . . . I have always been a conservative, Bible believing Baptist Christian. But I will not bow my knee to any Baptist bishop. . . ."

Mission work, an area Jimmy had a long-established concern for, was one area where the ideological conflict scarcely penetrated. Jimmy never shied away from any argument, but it must have been a pleasant change to travel far away from the political maneuverings and deal with problems that were so much more basic and simple to understand.

Ever since his first mission trip in 1973 to Brazil and Argentina, Jimmy had committed time and resources to world outreach. In 1986 he invited a missionary from Kenya to speak to the church one April Sunday night. The man was in the U. S. on medical leave for surgery on his leg. Speaking to an audience of about two hundred, the missionary said he and his team were looking for forty people to come to Mombasa, Kenya, on August 1, less than four months away.

After he finished his appeal, Brother Jimmy told the group, "I think this is God's invitation to us." Then, turning to the missionary, he said, "We'll have forty people there August 1." It was a statement made in faith, with no idea of how they could find that many volunteers and get all the travel plans confirmed in so short a time. With God's help, they arrived in Mombasa on time—with forty-seven volunteers ready to work.

When Jimmy preached the first Sunday morning at First Baptist Church of Mombasa, fifty-two people responded with professions of faith. Draper and the church pastor took a bullhorn to a nearby crossroad and preached some more, then preached and talked individually to people as they walked the streets. Jimmy suddenly realized, "We don't need to preach just in the church. We need to preach in the street!"

Mombasa is an ancient seaport on the Indian Ocean and the traditional gateway to the country from the east. The city, with a population approaching half a million, is built on an island, and Jimmy noticed the traffic on the street leading to the ferry pier was always heavy. He and his Kenyan colleague parked a flatbed truck on the path to the ferry landing, fired up the bullhorn, and started preaching. Others in the group made an impromptu puppet theater out of sheets and started working with their puppets. Crowds gathered by the hundreds; many had never seen a puppet before and were as fascinated by the process as by the message. In a week of street preaching Jimmy and the group received more than six thousand professions of faith.

His experience in Africa left a special place in Jimmy's heart for missionary outreach there, and he went back many times, each trip producing great work for Christ and wonderful memories. He led a group back in 1986 and another in 1987, when he went to the Kenyan city of Kitale, more than 450 miles inland near the Ugandan border. There was an exceptionally creative and resourceful missionary there planning a ministry to the Pokot tribe, one of the most primitive tribes in the country. The Kenyan authorities wouldn't let them travel with cameras, so they left them at an army checkpoint. Later they came to a river and had to cross on foot. The water was clear and only knee deep, so they took off their shoes, rolled up their pants, and waded across without any trouble.

In the time they were there, Jimmy and his associates established three churches in the wilderness. One village where they preached was attacked six weeks later by invading tribesmen; all the men and boys were murdered. Yet Jimmy and his group never felt threatened or fearful; rather they felt the protection of Christ around them every step of the way.

The next year, the missionary they had worked with in Kitale came to the United States on furlough and brought a video of a baptism in the same river Jimmy and the others had waded across. Before the ceremony, the tape showed two men wading out into the water and putting sticks in the river bottom. Jimmy asked what the sticks were for. The missionary explained that the baptisms were during the rainy season when the river rose. The river flowed into Lake Turkana, the most heavily crocodile-infested place in Kenya. When the river was high, crocodiles swam up into the river. The people gathered on the bank to watch prayed that no crocodiles would come into the area between sticks while the baptisms were going on. This challenge was in addition to the fact that many Africans, living in dry areas, had never been wet all over in their lives and were terrified of water. The act of baptism was a profession of faith far beyond what the American visitors could have imagined.

Even recreation gave Jimmy the chance to preach the gospel in Africa. In 1988 he and Terry Horton, a layman at Euless, were preaching in Mombasa and got the opportunity to spend a few days hunting. They flew inland on the small missionary plane dubbed "Baptist Air," then drove to a little place called Mutuwambu, meaning "Mosquito River."

They stopped for gas, and one of the missionaries with them said, "We need to preach here."

"Why?" Jimmy asked.

"Because we haven't preached all day!"

They weren't allowed to preach at the gas station, but the attendant suggested they go to the town market, where the crowd would be much bigger anyway. They pulled their vehicle up near the market vendors, stood on the tailgate, and Jimmy pushed a button on the bullhorn that made it play "The Eyes of Texas." A crowd immediately gathered, and the men began sharing the gospel.

After they finished, one listener, a tall man who happened to be an African Christian, told them he had been praying for someone to start a church in Mutuwambu and he wanted to help. His request was the first in a chain of events that showed new evidence of God's power to build His church.

Jimmy and his party spent the night at the East African Seminary in Arusha, Tanzania, where they visited a student named Benjamin who was being sponsored by a member of Jimmy's church back in Euless. Benjamin said he loved the seminary, but wanted to preach and start a church. The next morning at breakfast, their host's wife said, "Somebody gave us money to start a church in Mutuwambu but we don't have anybody who can go up there and preach."

"Have we got a deal for you!" Jimmy exclaimed sitting at the breakfast table. He explained the events of the previous day and the offer of the man to help start a church. In short order the money, the seminary student, a strong supporter, and the opportunity in Mutuwambu were transformed into a new church.

"Every day I was in East Africa was like that in one way or another," Jimmy later recalled. "You'd sit down at the end of the day and say, 'Wow, look what God led us to do.'" He witnessed to soldiers who gave up their careers to follow Christ. One new Christian named Mohammed wanted a new name to go with his new faith. "I'll give you my name, James, if you like," Jimmy said, and the man gratefully agreed.

Jimmy's personal ministry in Africa culminated in 1990 with the Mombasa Kenya Coast Crusade, when he led 536 people from eighty-three churches in sixteen states on a month-long trip to preach, teach, witness, and evangelize. Every day of the trip Jimmy saw evidence of God's hand. By the time their work was done, Jimmy and his team recorded nearly seventy thousand professions of faith. The last Sunday of the crusade there was a parade from the biggest Baptist church in Mombasa to the Indian Ocean. There, standing chest-deep in water where a shark had attacked two swimmers the week before, more than a dozen pastors, including Jimmy, baptized people simultaneously for three hours. At the end of the day more than one thousand Africans celebrated their new life in Christ as baptized believers.

In a five-year period Jimmy spent seventeen weeks overseas, twelve of them in Kenya, preaching, witnessing, encouraging missionaries, and reporting back to the congregation in Euless what their prayers and resources were accomplishing for God in every corner of the world.

But later in 1990, having avoided deadly tribal warfare year after year on the Kenya/Uganda/Sudan border, Jimmy found himself face-to-face with another kind of factional conflict much closer to home.

CHAPTER 19

OUT OF THE
FRYING PAN

IN 1990, JIMMY DRAPER was elected chairman of the board of trustees of Southwestern Seminary with its outspoken anti-conservative president, but it was down the road at his other alma mater in Waco that the most stunning shot was fired in the continuing denominational controversy.

At a media luncheon on the Baylor campus on September 5, university president Herbert Reynolds told the press that "Baptist fundamentalists" were making an "extremely serious" effort to take over Baylor. The next day the *Fort Worth Star-Telegram* reported:

> Fundamentalists have criticized Baylor's religion faculty as being too liberal, lambasted Reynolds for not firing a Mormon professor, and have charged that the school is becoming too worldly and moving away from strict Christian teaching.

> Reynolds, one of the most forceful critics of fundamentalist leaders, contends that they want to squelch

religious and academic freedom. He recently compared
the fundamentalist power tactics to those used by
Hitler's Third Reich.

The paper went on to add:

> Reynolds did not answer directly when asked if
> Baylor trustees might vote to withdraw from the
> Baptist General Convention of Texas if they saw the
> state convention (which appointed Baylor's trustees
> and funded part of its budget) gradually coming under
> fundamentalist control.
>
> "The trustees and I and others did not come to
> town on a load of hay," he said, "and we will do those
> things which we hope will be the right thing for the
> institution in the years to come."

Unlike the six Southern Baptist seminaries, Baylor, the largest
and most prestigious Baptist university, was not controlled by the
Southern Baptist Convention but by the Baptist General
Convention of Texas. The BGCT had not voted in conservative
leadership to the same extent as the SBC.

Jimmy Draper's reaction to Reynolds' veiled threat appeared in
the *Dallas Times Herald* on September 7 in a section front page
story headlined, "No coup at Baylor, top Baptists vow."

> Leaders of the fundamentalist side of the great
> Southern Baptist schism expressed hurt, surprise and
> ignorance Thursday at charges by Baylor University
> President Herbert Reynolds that they plan to take over
> the state convention and then Baylor.
>
> "It's all part of the Chicken Little mentality: If you
> can keep everyone thinking the sky is falling, you keep
> them scared and on your side" said Jimmy Draper, a
> fundamentalist pastor of First Baptist Church in Euless.

"He's been claiming that for years, but I know of no planned attempt to take over Baylor or the convention," he said.

Two weeks to the day after that statement, there was a takeover at Baylor, but it was nothing like Jimmy Draper or any of the other conservative leaders could have anticipated.

On Friday, September 21, 1990, the Baylor Board of Trustees voted to change the charter of the university, transferring "sole management and control" of the institution to a self-sustaining board of regents. Henceforth only 25 percent of the trustees, rather than the previous 100 percent, would come from the state convention and 75 percent from the regents themselves.

The official news release from the Baylor Department of Communications quoted Reynolds in his moment of triumph:

"This is an historic and courageous initiative by the Board of Trustees. This action will maintain Baylor's academic excellence and continue its world-wide Christian emphasis. Friends, students and alumni of Baylor can be assured that Baylor will remain true to its historic mission of being the world's finest Christian university and, at the same time, be free from an attempted takeover by any special interest group."

The Baylor Alumni Association published a pamphlet that took a more direct view of events:

"On September 21 Baylor University trustees, while resolutely affirming the university's historic affiliation with Texas Baptists, took action that removes the threat of a political takeover by Presslerite-Fundamentalists, or any other extremist group.

"By altering the university charter, Baylor trustees created a separate governing body that will not be controlled by the Baptist General Convention of Texas (BGCT). . . .

"The move was made to thwart a threatened takeover of the university by Presslerite-Fundamentalists who, in the wake of their 12th consecutive victory at the SBC level [electing Morris Chapman to the presidency in New Orleans the previous summer], had targeted a takeover of the Baptist General Convention of Texas, with Baylor one of the primary goals.

"'Baylor will no longer be a political prize for extremist groups to covet,' said Mike Bishop, vice president for university communications."

To a reporter for the *Houston Chronicle*, Jimmy called the action at Baylor "a modern-day act of piracy. This does help explain, though, why some of the attacks on some of us [conservatives] have been so vicious by the administration of Baylor. They had to have this appearance of siege in order to do this."

The afternoon the trustees voted, a lawyer stood by at the state capitol in Austin with a phone in his hand, waiting for instructions. As soon as the votes were cast, he got the word and, as had been prearranged, dashed in to file the new charter with the Texas secretary of state just before the office closed. None of Reynolds' opponents knew anything about the plan until it was too late to stop it.

Soon afterward, Jimmy spoke to the controversy in an installment of "From My Heart to Yours," his column in the church newsletter. After relating what had happened and the Baylor trustees' reasons for it, Jimmy commented:

THAT IS A DIRECT REVERSAL OF EVERY PRINCIPLE BAPTISTS HAVE EVER HELD HISTORICALLY! Trustees have been for over one hundred years elected by the BGCT to hold the property and management of that university in trust for the convention. The consenting trustees were guilty of a brazen and unprecedented breach of fiduciary responsibility and, in effect, voted to steal the assets of the University from the very Convention which has selected them to safeguard them.

If such action were to take place in the business world, where a corporate board of directors took over a corporation for themselves and dispossessed the stockholders, such action would prompt criminal, as well as civil, prosecution.

[President Reynolds and the trustees] expect Texas Baptists to continue sending money and students, but have nothing significant to do with the operation of the school. Such action and attitude is inexcusable and unacceptable to Texas Baptists. . . .

I raise my voice now in opposition to this action by the Baylor Trustees. I agree with our *Baptist Standard* editor, Dr. Presnall Wood, when he called this action 'a slap at all Texas Baptists,' 'disrespectful and disappointing,' 'a betrayal of a long relationship of Baylor with Texas Baptists' and that it 'should be questioned and opposed.'

Ending his column on a positive note, Jimmy wrote, "WHAT A GREAT SEPTEMBER GOD GAVE US! SEE YOU SUNDAY AS WE BEGIN A NEW CHURCH YEAR THAT WILL BE THE GREATEST YET!"

It would be Jimmy's sixteenth year as pastor of First Baptist Church of Euless–the year of the Mombasa Kenya Coast

Crusade, of sustained growth in the church, of new challenges as the chairman of trustees at Southwestern Seminary.

And after thirty-five years in the pulpit and leading a congregation, it would be his last as a full-time pastor.

Draper's service as SBC president during two of its most divisive years, as chairman of trustees at Southwestern, his previous trustee appointments at Baylor and the Annuity Board, his nearly two dozen books, and his unqualified success at building the church at Euless all brought his name to the attention of a group of men who weren't looking for a pastor but for a leader of another stripe.

They were members of the search committee seeking a new president for the Sunday School Board, the largest SBC entity, one of the most complex, and one with a daunting leadership crisis.

The Sunday School Board was organized by the SBC in 1891 to produce Bible study materials. Beginning with materials for children, it quickly grew to publishing Bible studies for all ages. Over the years, books, Bibles, hymnals, magazines, and audiovisuals were added, along with a wide range of services. By 1990, on the verge of its centennial, the Sunday School Board also oversaw a vast catalog of church supplies from leaflets to baptisteries, a nationwide chain of bookstores, conference centers in North Carolina and New Mexico, a music publishing venture, and other interests.

However, the Board was tracking on a downward trend. Unit sales in most categories had been on a decline for more than fifteen years. Trade books under the Broadman imprint and Baptist Book Stores were widely regarded as dated and not competitive with other Christian publishers and retailers. Dr. Lloyd Elder, who had led the Board since 1984, had reorganized the institution twice during his tenure but was unable to reverse the trends. These years were also the height of the denominational controversy, and frustration had mounted between many trustees and Elder.

The flashpoint came with the submission of a commissioned manuscript to Broadman Press. Entitled *Celebrating Heritage and Hope,* it was intended as the centennial history of the Board and was written by Jimmy's old friend and carpooler, Leon McBeth, professor of church history at Southwestern, who was also the frantic convention messenger that had confronted Jimmy and his brother Charlie on the sidewalk in Houston back in 1979.

As the manuscript came together in the summer and fall of 1989, Broadman editor Vicki Crumpton praised it to McBeth as "a fascinating story, written in your best style." Yet Crumpton went on to add that "quite often you go beyond the facts to make interpretations about causes, underlying motives, possible consequences, and so on." She said she softened these in her editing, but understood that the author and Dr. Elder had "discussed your freedom in writing this history" and that the BSSB president was comfortable with "evaluations and interpretations" as long as they were supported by facts.

McBeth replied in a letter that Crumpton's assumptions were right, and that Elder said that the Board wanted something more than a collection of historical data. McBeth said that Elder "specifically affirmed that the author should have freedom, and would have freedom, to interpret the data in the context of Southern Baptist history."

That freedom, according to interoffice memos of the time, resulted in a manuscript that was "heavily slanted in the anti-conservative way." It seemed that "the history written about living people [particularly Dr. Elder, as it turned out] was highly selective history . . . criticism could be raised that some of the living historical figures were allowed to interpret their own historical involvement while other significant persons were not even mentioned." There were also facts taken from confidential personnel files that would subject the publisher to libel action.

The manuscript underwent various revisions and was finally typeset in the summer of 1990, but as the typescript made its way through the approval process, resistance to publishing it mounted. A trustee subcommittee assigned to read the final text reported concerns about the way the author had handled the trustee meeting the year before when a motion to fire Elder had been made. After a series of meetings in August, the project was shelved. *Celebrating Heritage and Hope* was never published.

After continuing conflicts between Elder and the trustees, the general administration committee voted to remove Elder from his position during what Dr. Gene Mims, vice chairman of trustees, later described as "a very long, arduous, tension-filled meeting." On January 17, 1991, the trustees met again "for the purpose of evaluating and responding to the performance" of Elder. Two hours before the meeting, lawyers for the two sides reached an agreement that Elder would retire on January 31, 1992, or thirty days after a successor was named, whichever came first.

In February 1991 the chairman of trustees appointed a search committee, and the process began. Such a high-profile, high-powered job attracted many applicants, but very few had the combination of abilities the position required. The search committee decided early on that the best candidate would probably be a pastor. They believed it would take a pastor with excellent leadership and relational skills to connect with the thousands of congregations and millions of Southern Baptists who were the backbone of the Sunday School Board's market.

A friend of one of the search committee trustees called to suggest Jimmy Draper for the job. He was a well-respected and successful pastor who had served in several offices as a denominational leader, the caller noted. The committee added Draper's name to the list and, in time, took up the prospect of his candidacy for the job. It seemed to everyone that Jimmy's unique attribute was that he was well regarded in both the conservative and moderate camps. Even his opponents felt he was personable and fair. As one committee member observed, "He didn't draw any lightning" from any quarter.

Jimmy Draper had no interest in the job. He'd been preaching since he was fourteen and pastoring since he was twenty. His church was thriving, his congregation loved him and his family, and he expected to finish his career at First Baptist Euless. To encourage Draper to talk with the search committee, they asked him to meet them at the Dallas-Fort Worth airport and advise them on what kind of person would be best for the job. When Draper got to the meeting room and sat down, the members told him they were there to consider *him* for the job.

Up to that time Jimmy had been relaxed and calm in the room, observers said. But when he heard what the committee wanted, he pushed away the briefing folder in front of him and folded his arms. He didn't enjoy being taken so completely off guard and sincerely preferred to stay with his church-based ministry.

A few days later, after the friend who suggested Jimmy in the first place encouraged them to try again, a representative of the committee called Jimmy to ask him to meet with them once more. God had been at work in his heart, and he was now more open to the idea of leading the Sunday School Board.

The one complication was that by then the trustees had offered another man the job, and it was his to accept or turn down. In the end, that candidate declined the position, leaving the committee free to offer the job to Jimmy. He didn't think of himself as an administrator or corporate officer, but the search committee made clear the kind of leader they were seeking. "We wanted him to lead, motivate, inspire, paint the vision," said Gene Mims, a search committee member who later joined the Board as a vice president. "We weren't attracted to his skills; we were attracted to him as a person."

After receiving the committee's invitation, Jimmy followed his long-established pattern–especially when considering a move–of listening for the voice of God. Within a few weeks, he and Carol Ann decided once again to leave their friends (and this time their children and grandchildren as well) and head out to do the Lord's work in a new vineyard. The church at Euless was sad to lose a pastor they loved so much, but they knew it was God's will; otherwise, they were convinced Brother Jimmy would never have made the decision to go.

"Jimmy taught us how to act," one member explained. "He doesn't want to be anywhere except in the center of where God wants him to be." If God's will was for their pastor to move, it was up to them not to pout, but to celebrate. There was, a member recalled, "a real victory attitude." And so with flowers, tears, and heartfelt wishes, the church wished the Drapers Godspeed.

Jimmy's career accomplishments and his impeccable record as a pastor made him a great choice for the Sunday School Board. SBC moderates hadn't wanted Lloyd Elder to go, but if he had to leave, they were at least relieved that Jimmy Draper was going to replace him. In all the years of SBC turmoil, Jimmy had never burned a bridge. Dr. Mims remembered, "The tension was built up like a powder keg. We wanted the right individual, and when Jimmy's name came forth it was just right. It really was."

And so Jimmy left Euless for a new career at the Sunday School Board headquarters, an enormous complex in downtown

Nashville covering more than a million square feet. He had only been inside the place once before in his life. And he had never spent a day running a business, much less a $180-million-dollar one. To Jimmy it was more than a new job; it was a new identity. "I've always said being a pastor is not what I do but what I am," he said in a Baptist Press interview the morning after he had preached his last sermon in Euless.

Eager to get a handle on his new responsibilities, Jimmy sought advice about leading a large business and ministry enterprise even before he left Euless. One person he talked with was Mike Arrington, a member of his church and a vice president of Texas Utilities. As Jimmy and Carol Ann had prayed about their move, Jimmy felt God leading him to ask Mike and his wife, Paula, to make the move to Nashville and for Mike to put his business experience to work at the Sunday School Board.

"What I saw in Jimmy as a pastor that was as important in being here was that he was a person who was as Christlike as anybody I have ever known," said Arrington, who joined the Board and became vice president for corporate affairs. "He's not a dictator, but he is a coach, a person who allows people to accomplish all they can with his support and knowledge."

In his August 21 inaugural address Jimmy made clear to the audience of employees, trustees, and guests that he would not be satisfied with the status quo. "There ought to be a restless discontent with what we are as we look at where we ought to be. We ought to dream big." He envisioned an international presence bringing Sunday School Board resources to churches and Christians around the world.

He laid out four dimensions of leadership that would receive his attention: spiritual, business, organization, and people leadership. "It will be my task to try to give us a clear and compelling vision for us to aim at, to aspire to, and I will work hard at enabling necessary changes to be meaningful and to take hold," Jimmy pledged.

He would need such a vision as he prepared to lead the Sunday School Board through the years of dramatic change ahead.

CHAPTER 20

WINDS OF CHANGE

W HEN JIMMY AND CAROL ANN moved into a rented house in Nashville in August 1991, Jimmy's mother remained in Euless. By the time she joined her son and daughter-in-law a few months later, a family friend had also made herself an indispensable part of the household.

Mary Betts was a member of the church in Euless who felt God's calling to move to Nashville along with the Drapers. She accepted a position in prayer ministry at the Sunday School Board and also became caregiver to Lois Draper, with whom she had developed a special friendship over the past several years. Mary moved into the Drapers' home and found real joy in helping Grandmother around the house, preparing meals, and keeping her company while the Drapers were traveling. She referred to herself with a chuckle as the "Granny Nanny."

In the home the Drapers built in Brentwood, a suburb just south of Nashville, Grandmother had her own quiet suite on the second floor and an elevator ran from the basement garage up to the hallway outside her bedroom, enabling her easy access to the whole house. The first floor was designed around an open concept, and Carol Ann accented the rooms with souvenirs of their mission trips to South America and Africa. In his spacious study, Jimmy hung a row of mounted trophies from his annual deer hunts with son Bailey.

Organizing a new household was simple compared with the task awaiting Jimmy at the Sunday School Board. Immersing himself in the recent history and performance of the corporation, Jimmy concluded that creative, innovative strategic ideas were in short supply. Productivity suffered and the general work ethic was below par. He sought out the counsel of Dr. James L. Sullivan, who headed the Sunday School Board from 1953 to 1975. In September 1991 Sullivan handed Jimmy six handwritten pages outlining his administrative philosophy in 44 points, beginning with this admonition: "A person who steps out of the pastorate into a denominational job steps down. It matters not how high or big the position." Sullivan also offered a memorable metaphor for crisis times: "Patience is especially helpful in controversy or crisis times. Did you ever get mushy mud on your clothes? If you tried to brush it off immediately, all you did was smear it. Give it a little time, and it dries into dust. Then you can brush it off easily and move on." His concluding advice, "Have fun!"

After a period of study and counsel with an executive consulting firm, Jimmy resolved to bring in experienced, innovative leaders to pull the Board out of its slump. Five of the six vice presidents were, like Draper, ministers without experience in a business environment.

The more he saw, the more Jimmy believed that many people at the Board had the potential to be valuable employees, but they needed to be challenged to work more creatively and efficiently, then given the resources to do so. The Board's performance was lackluster and had been for years. The bookstores were outdated, and the conference centers needed refurbishing; both were losing money. The trade publishing business brought only a trickle of net proceeds. The only significant income came from the substantial profits on curriculum and church supplies.

The challenges he faced had deep roots. Not only were the bookstores behind the times, too many were in the wrong parts of town. Trade books needed more polish on the inside as well as the outside. At its most fundamental, Jimmy knew revitalizing the Board was a matter not of products and service, but of personal ministry among Christian brothers and sisters. As leader of the Board, Jimmy realized he needed to be out front building relationships on behalf of the organization. As he spoke to employees and to Southern Baptists across the country, his consistent message was that the future of the Sunday School Board and of the Southern Baptist Convention depended upon relationships.

While Jimmy had no experience as a business executive, his career in ministry had prepared him for the task at hand in important ways. As a member of several boards of trustees he had gained experience in resource allocation, employee relations, and fiscal management. As president of a contentious SBC he had refined the art of negotiation and reconciliation without betraying his principles. Perhaps most important of all, he knew from thirty-five years as a pastor that almost all problems are people problems at their core, and that by supporting, encouraging, admonishing, equipping, rewarding—and occasionally replacing—people, virtually any problem could be solved. Recognizing that her husband was facing challenges beyond any he had dealt with before, Carol Ann prayed every morning, "Please, Lord, let him know things he can't possibly know."

Jimmy's range of past experience taught him the value of advice from men and women in the ranks who faced the challenges of the

Sunday School Board every day. Early in his presidency, the Senior Executive Team organized four employee task forces to study the structure of the organization, how the company did business and ministry, what worked and what didn't, what communications strategies were needed, and how to change and improve in the future. Task force members were not Board officers, but supervisors and line workers in the thick of the operation.

The groups worked four months and then came back with specific recommendations, which Jimmy and his team began acting on immediately. One task force proposed a restructuring to focus more on the needs of churches and people, improving product quality, and promoting greater flexibility. Another group recommended downsizing and proposed an early retirement option with special financial incentives. Though only certain positions would be eliminated, the law required the Board to offer the same package to everyone qualified by age and tenure. The rule of thumb was that about 30 percent of employees offered early retirement would take it. But of the 191 eligible employees, more than 80 percent accepted. While some employees felt they were being shoved out, others were glad for the generous package. One of Jimmy's few regrets about the restructuring was losing some employees he sincerely wanted to keep.

Past Board presidents were traditionally seen as aloof and not inclined to socialize with the rank and file. One of Jimmy's first official acts was to move his office from the walnut-paneled suite on the eleventh floor to a new location just off a busy ground-floor hallway between the main entrance and the cafeteria. He was accessible and committed to feeling the day-to-day pulse of the organization. Employees soon learned his door was open to them, and he returned their phone calls and answered their e-mails. Over time, he challenged them to grant the same kind of accessibility to each other, to Southern Baptists at large, to ministry partners, and others.

Under Jimmy's leadership, the Senior Executive Team began filling management positions with experts in their fields. Ted Warren, a committed Christian layman who had spent twenty-two years in the oil business and headed two companies, was named vice president for finance. Ken Stephens, an executive with a Nashville publishing company, came to lead the trade publishing division. Mike Harry left a prestigious job as director of distribution for Neiman-Marcus to take on that role for the Board. Janice Bell, who honed her customer service skills at a major airline, came to run a similar program in the Church Resources Division. The team also proudly promoted leaders from within. Mark Scott moved up from the ranks, first to interim director of the Book Store Division and later to vice president of the Retail Division. Building a world-class organization took world-class people, and Jimmy Draper and his leadership team were dedicated to finding them.

Jimmy sensed a strong current of loyalty and set out to change the culture by nurturing it. He saw in employee loyalty to previous leaders the potential to be loyal to his administration, remembering his father's admonition about churches and pastors, "Son, don't be threatened if the people love their former pastor. That means they have the capacity to love you." Drawing on his own experience, Jimmy added, "You can't buy loyalty. It's a character trait. You can't make people happy by what you give them. They're either loyal or they're not."

After a time of adjustment people began to warm to Jimmy's leadership approach. Pastoral experience had taught him that people have to feel like they know someone before they can trust him. There were faithful supporters of the previous administration who initially resented the changes taking place. But most of those feelings dissolved as they began to see Jimmy's style of leadership.

He wanted to build a climate where people could be challenged to do their best, get the right training, and feel satisfaction and fulfillment in their work. He wanted to challenge employees to take risks and be willing to make mistakes in order to find new and better ways of working.

To clarify mission and purpose, the Senior Executive Team set out to craft a vision statement. The first vision of the Draper administration focused on high-quality products and processes, which the leadership team identified as the most important needs. That vision stated: "*We will assist local churches and believers to evangelize the world to Christ, develop believers, and grow churches by being the best worldwide provider of relevant, high-quality, high-value Christian products and services.*"

Within a few years the processes were dramatically improved and the products approaching world class. By 1996 every facet of operations was new from the ground up, from Sunday School lesson design to book store operations to warehouse management. The first vision was now realized. It was time to move to a new vision that was more strategic and spiritual in nature: "*As God works through us, we will help people and churches know Jesus Christ and seek His Kingdom by providing biblical solutions that spiritually transform individuals and cultures.*"

During those busy, productive years of transformation, Jimmy also transformed the relationship between the president and the trustees. As he had done as a pastor and as SBC president, he reached out to get to know them personally, laid out direction in his messages at their semiannual meetings, and answered their questions thoughtfully, building bonds of partnership and trust that had frayed during previous administrations.

As part of that building process, the trustees had to focus on their role as "big picture" thinkers and strategists, resisting the temptation to take on day-to-day administrative responsibilities. Having reestablished an atmosphere of trust between the president and the Board, the two then moved on to establish credibility with Southern Baptist Convention leaders and Southern Baptists at large. Kirk Humphreys, a layman and former mayor of Oklahoma City who also chaired the Board of Trustees, believed Jimmy "dramatically repositioned the Sunday School Board. He made the tough decision to restructure and refocus. Yes, it's a business, but it's also ministry." On a personal note he added, "I know Jimmy Draper loves me, and I know there are thousands of people who feel that way."

Draper also worked with dedication to strengthen relationships and cooperation with presidents of other SBC entities. Bob Reccord, president of the North American Mission Board, first met Jimmy in 1974 as a student at Southwestern Seminary when Jimmy was associate pastor of First Baptist Church, Dallas. "I'll never forget the gracious kindness with which Dr. Draper embraced me and made me feel like I was the only thing on his agenda for the day," Reccord recalled. Years later Jimmy helped him decide how to respond to the offer that he be recommended as president of the NAMB. Draper offered to fly to Virginia with Carol Ann to meet Reccord and his wife, Cheryl, and spend a day "talking about what it is like to make a significant transition from the pastor of a local church to the president of a Southern Baptist entity. . . . It was one of the most beneficial and helpful days Cheryl and I would have in the decision process through which we were moving."

Jimmy made strengthening relationships with state convention leaders another high priority. In his first three years as president, he visited every state convention headquarters, spending a full day in listening sessions with the state executive director and his staff. He brought back questions and made sure responses went out within a week. Jimmy considered these visits among the best investments of his time in those early years.

Dr. John Sullivan, executive director-treasurer of the Florida Baptist Convention, first worked closely with Jimmy when he was SBC president and Sullivan was first vice president. "He was always fair, but never weak," Sullivan said. "Someone coined the phrase, 'a velvet brick.' That's Draper under pressure. There is no executive at the SBC level more respected than Jimmy Draper. To my knowledge he is the only executive at the national level that has, by his design, visited in the office of every executive director in the SBC. He comes without an agenda and talks through our issues. But that is who Jimmy Draper is."

While Jimmy was closely involved with many strategic initiatives of the Board, he separated himself from preparing the annual corporate financial statements, not seeing them until they were complete. When complimented about leading the Sunday School Board into the black, Jimmy responded with a smile, "They were in the black when I got here. First, I led them into the red and then back into the black!"

In 1993–94 the Board reported a loss of $8.3 million due to a write-off of old expenses and costs that had lingered on the books for years. This and other continuing challenges prompted Jimmy to make another key organizational change in his leadership team, a decision he reached while traveling in Korea. When he returned, he announced he was elevating Ted Warren from vice president for finance to executive vice president and chief operating officer. Other vice presidents would then report to Warren.

This freed Jimmy to major on his strength of building relationships on behalf of the Sunday School Board.

"My skills are business, administration, understanding the numbers, understanding how to organize and operate a large company of this size," Warren said. "Jimmy's skills are on the people side, church life, denomination life. He loves to preach and speak and know everybody. We're certainly not redundant. We bring those differences together to make a pretty good unit."

After a decade as chief operating officer, Warren described his partnership with Jimmy: "I stay here most of the time and worry about what's going on inside. That frees him up to have his mind and his heart on the churches, the denomination, the external affairs." He notes that this kind of working relationship is common in the business world.

As the Draper administration progressed, Baptist Book Stores became one of the first targets for a major overhaul. After being named interim division director at 33, Mark Scott said Jimmy challenged him and his leadership team to do their best, gave them the freedom to fail, and empowered them to fix what wasn't working. They started slowly, working one store at a time, deciding whether to relocate, remodel, or close the store. Most stores fell into the first two categories. In the process, the team introduced dramatic technological improvements along with better product selection, more competitive pricing, and more responsive customer service, and created a spiritually uplifting atmosphere in the stores so that hundreds of people are now led to accept Christ as their Savior there every year. To enter markets with small numbers of Southern Baptists, Scott launched a new initiative, purchasing existing stores and converting them to Baptist Bookstores. At the end of 2004, the chain had almost doubled to 122 stores with revenue of $218 million, more than the income of the entire Sunday School Board in 1991.

"Jimmy helped protect us to give us the time to fix what wasn't working and then he helped provide the funding," Scott said. "If we could present our case, I cannot think of a single time he turned us down. He held us accountable for results. Our challenge then was to deliver what we promised, and he supported us in that."

Jimmy's hand also helped redirect the Board's publishing division. Broadman Press, viewed by many as a vanity press for Southern Baptist pastors and professors, embraced a new commitment to quality. In 1993, the Broadman imprint was merged with the Board's Holman Bible publishers, the oldest Bible publisher in America, to form Broadman & Holman. Within a decade of Jimmy's arrival as president, a book carrying the B&H imprint appeared on the *New York Times* best-seller list--*Payne Stewart: The Authorized Biography* by Tracey Stewart with Ken Abraham. B&H books also were regularly nominated for Gold Medallion Awards, given annually by the Evangelical Christian Publishers Association.

The Church Resources Division released acclaimed interactive discipleship course books by well-known authors, including Henry Blackaby, T. W. Hunt, Beth Moore, Ann Graham Lotz, and Joni Eareckson Tada. Their newly redesigned Vacation Bible School materials prompted an enthusiastic response.

In historical perspective, offering the job of BSSB president to Jimmy Draper carried a high element of risk: as a corporate executive he was an unknown quantity. Accepting the job had a correspondent risk for Draper: it meant leaving a comfortable, successful career in middle age to sail through unknown and choppy seas. In God's providence the combination of the man with the job was the best fit imaginable. Jimmy guided the corporation on to new heights of achievement using the collective skills that had somehow been preparing him for this leadership role all along.

Within a few years Jimmy had become as respected for leading the Board through a time of massive change and influencing new directions within the denomination as he had been as a pastor for achievements in the pulpit and on the mission field. The changing seasons also brought changes in his and Carol Ann's personal life. The number of grandchildren increased to six: Randy and Elizabeth's children, Kyle and Kevin; Bailey and Kim's children, Jon and James; and Terri and Mike's (Wilkinson) children, Wes and Leigh Ann.

And there was another change. By 1996, Lois Draper's health had deteriorated to the point where it was no longer possible for her to live safely at home. She moved into an assisted living home in nearby Franklin. Ever grateful and gracious, she never resisted or resented the move. The following year when Jimmy and Carol Ann were in Ashland, Kentucky, they got a call saying Grandmother's life was nearing its close. They hurried to the Cincinnati airport, where bad weather delayed them for hours. When they finally arrived back in Nashville, Grandmother was still alive. The nurses said they believed she was hanging on until they got there. And so Jimmy and Carol Ann were with his mother to say good-bye, with gratitude for Lois Draper's lifelong example of Christian faith, service, and love.

CHAPTER 21

AND NEW THINGS HAVE COME

F IVE YEARS INTO THE DRAPER administration, the Sunday School Board had become a completely renewed and revitalized organization with products, state-of-the-art distribution, a top leadership team, and a bright future ahead. Some in the organization felt a new name was in order too. They thought that the Sunday School Board no longer reflected the institution's broad scope of ministries. They pressed for a new name with a stronger spiritual reference that was also versatile enough to be part of the names of business units. That way, they said, customers could better understand the whole range of products and services the Board provided. Surveys through the years regularly had shown that church leaders and customers who bought SSB literature, shopped in Baptist Book Stores, owned a Broadman book or Holman Bible, and attended conferences at Glorieta (N.M.) and Ridgecrest (N.C.) conference centers had no idea all of these ministries were part of one organization.

Mike Arrington, vice president for corporate affairs, was the first member of the Senior Executive Team to promote the change five months into the Draper administration. Arrington recalled a meeting where Jimmy and the vice presidents went around the table listing key issues they felt they should address in the next five years.

"I said we needed to look at a name change," Arrington recalled. The idea was shelved at the time as other concerns demanded immediate attention. However, by 1996 the time seemed right to at least explore the possibility of changing the name of the 105-year-old Sunday School Board.

Jimmy, usually a strong advocate for change, was hesitant regarding the name. "My first reaction was, it's like moving a country graveyard—you can't do it," he recalled later. "I felt like the Sunday School Board was so well established in the minds of people that it would be hard to acclimate them to something else without a lot of trauma. At the beginning I wasn't convinced it was necessary."

Even so, Jimmy agreed to have a task force study the idea and make recommendations. As the study progressed Jimmy gradually became convinced a name change was in order after James L. Sullivan, Draper's predecessor and mentor, supported the idea, noting that when the SBC began adding ministries outside of Sunday School to its portfolio in the early twentieth century the name had become outdated.

After working with an outside firm, surveying customer groups, and considering dozens of possibilities, three finalists were recommended by the task force. The first was Christian Ministry Resources, deemed appropriately descriptive but bland. Also, because it lacked a proprietary word it was impossible to copyright. The second proposal was Church Street Christian

Resources, which never gained traction with senior management. The third proposal was LifeWay Christian Resources, a reference to John 14:6 where Jesus said, "I am the way, the truth, and the life. No one comes to the Father except through me" (HCSB).

The LifeWay name steadily gained steam and built a following within the Board. LifeWay had first been used in the 1970s for two bookstores that later closed. It resurfaced in the early 1990s as a name for select stores in markets with few Southern Baptists and as a printing imprint. The full name became LifeWay Christian Resources of the Southern Baptist Convention. Soon after final approval in 1998, the Church Resources Division became LifeWay Church Resources, Baptist Book Stores became LifeWay Christian Stores, and Glorieta and Ridgecrest conference centers became LifeWay Glorieta and LifeWay Ridgecrest. The Web site became www.lifeway.com.

"Frankly," Jimmy said in retrospect, "it's been probably the best thing we've done. It opened up doors that we would never have opened before. We had one area where the developer would not let us put in a Baptist Book Store. We changed to LifeWay Christian Stores, and they came to us and said they wanted a store. The only thing that changed was the name."

Using technology, especially the Internet, to enhance communication was another area the Draper administration addressed. In April 2000, Tim Vineyard, vice president of a firm specializing in computer, networking, and Internet services, came in to expand LifeWay's use of the Internet. In 2002 he became vice president of the Technology Division and chief information officer. Vineyard spearheaded improving the quality of the Web site and adding a long list of services, including online Bible study and Web sites for churches.

In 1997, Jimmy and the Executive Management Group began sponsoring mission trips, giving LifeWay employees time off to serve in the mission field and paying half their expenses. The trips, Draper explained, were to help employees see that "the work they do here has worldwide implications. I think it's helped us get our eyes off ourselves. It's helped us to see beyond the resources we produce and given us a greater sense of involvement in and responsibility for the Great Commission and sharing the gospel."

While the Sunday School Board began with the single mission of publishing Bible study materials, the Board had never owned the rights to a Bible translation. Holman published Bibles in a variety of translations, but had to pay royalties to do so. Also, the threat of possible changes to one popular translation by its owner in the name of "diversity" and "inclusiveness" underscored the value to the Board of an accurate, readable translation from the original languages that it could control. In 1998, with Jimmy's strong support, the Broadman & Holman Division joined forces with a Bible translation project that had begun in 1984. The translation, taken from the ancient Hebrew, Greek, and Aramaic by a 78-person team of translation scholars, was named the Holman Christian Standard Bible; the New Testament was released in 2001 and the complete Bible in 2004.

Jimmy continued to receive denominational honors and represent Southern Baptists to audiences across the world. In addition to his honorary doctorates from Howard Payne University (1974), Dallas Baptist University (1982), and Campbell University (1983), he was honored with a D.D. degree from California Baptist University in 2003. Jimmy was accorded a signal honor in 1995 when his alma mater, Southwestern Seminary, announced the establishment of the endowed James T. Draper, Jr., Chair of Pastoral Ministries. Southern Seminary presented him their highest honor in 1998, the E. Y. Mullins Distinguished Denominational Service Award. He was named in 1999 the recipient of the L. R. Scarborough Award honoring pastors, ministerial staff members, and denominational leaders influential in the life of Southwestern Seminary.

After twelve years as president, Jimmy Draper had built LifeWay into a $400+ million annual business and was as excited about looking for ways to improve the organization as he had been his first day on the job. When asked what he thought was the greatest challenge LifeWay would face over the next few years, he was quick to answer.

"The big thing is the delivery system. Technology has dramatically reduced the need for giant warehouses. We've got one in Nashville three blocks long that we've turned into office space. We'll always need some inventory and some human oversight, but our biggest opportunity for improving our service and improving our operating efficiency is in technology.

"In 2002 we sent out almost 21 million packages, but we have 30 to 40 percent fewer people in the warehouse than we had five years ago. Technology is changing the way we communicate and how we deliver our products. We can now pull an order, box it up, weigh it, put postage on it, and ship it out the door completely automatically.

"I think the biggest challenge is not being blown away by the technology but to manage it in a way that's helpful. Not everything the technological teams come up with will work, so we need people who can see well enough to make new technology and advancement our slave, not our master. With digital print-on-demand we can reprint out-of-print books in two weeks. We can deliver text on the Internet. The challenge there is how to keep the business solvent by figuring out how much to charge. Most of our creative and editorial expenses are the same regardless of the distribution method, so the big question moving forward will be, How do we charge for it, and how do we get paid?"

Another fundamental shift Jimmy detected was the dramatic change in the way churches minister to their congregations and plan their programs. "In the past lessons were all a quarter long," he explained. "Now we have lessons that run nine weeks or six weeks or less. This is changing how people run church programs. Newer, innovative churches want shorter lessons. We had a MasterLife campaign back in the 1980s that ran twenty-six weeks. Recently we split it up into four units of six weeks each. Staying abreast of how people are willing to learn, maximizing their time, is another key to future success. You'd think the more advanced we became the more time we'd have. But what's happening is that the more advanced we get, the more distractions we have. People want to do more in less time, and we have to design products at LifeWay that help them do that."

On September 3, 2000, Jimmy marked the fiftieth anniversary of his first sermon at First Baptist Church of Mixon, Texas. Reflecting on that half century of ministry, he shared twenty-one lessons he had learned. These lessons are as good a summary of his career as could be written and a fitting testimony to a lifetime spent growing more like Christ:

1. *Don't neglect your personal walk with the Lord.* No one will make time for you to stay fresh and growing in your relationship with the Lord if you don't. If you neglect this you'll be doing the work of God, but not the will of God.

2. *Make time for your family.* I put my wife and children on my appointment calendar and hold those dates as faithfully as any other. Don't care for everyone else and lose your family.

3. *Practice the ministry of encouragement.* My dad always reminded me to be kind to everybody, because everybody is having a hard time. Kindness and sensitivity to those you serve is vital.

4. *Never make a decision when you are discouraged or depressed.* If you do, you will seldom make the right decision.

5. *When your heart is right with God and you are confident in that relationship, understand that doubt never means yes.* It always means no or wait. God doesn't lead us through doubt.

6. *Be open and honest.* Be the same person in public as you are in private. It's worth the risk to be transparent. Some people will take advantage of that, but for most, it will be the key to effective ministry.

7. *Always return your phone calls and answer your mail.* This is a small thing that will bring great rewards as it sharpens your discipline and enhances your relationships. No one is important enough to be unresponsive to others.

8. *Don't let anger be a pattern of your behavior.* Treat people with courtesy, especially those who disagree with you. Firmness need not be brutal.

9. *Be quick to forgive mistakes, and work with people to help them avoid repeating them.* I don't know anyone who makes mistakes on purpose. Don't be hostile to those who make mistakes. You will need forgiveness and correction yourself.

10. *Let your preaching flow from the Bible.* Don't pick topics, then hunt for Scripture to substantiate your message. Start with Scripture. Careful, regular Bible study will always keep you on the cutting edge of both Scripture and contemporary needs.

11. *Always be prepared to preach.* Most people will see you only in the pulpit, so always be ready to give a word from God. You will have to fight for that time, and you must. It took me twenty-five to thirty hours of preparation every week to prepare the messages I preached during thirty-five years as a pastor.

12. *Don't flirt with temptation.* Determine now that you will not allow yourself to do things that will discredit you or the Lord. Don't wait until you are tempted to take a stand against temptation.

13. *Cooperate with your fellow believers.* None of us can fulfill the Great Commission by ourselves. The year after I was president of the SBC I served as vice chairman of the Tarrant Baptist Association, and the chairman was a pastor who had once been my intern. I didn't feel I'd taken a step down, but I was simply exercising the privilege of cooperation with fellow believers.

14. *Be a steward of your position and influence.* Whatever God has brought into your life and ministry, whatever He has allowed you to do, whatever success you have had, whatever disappointments and failures you have endured, all form a tapestry of experience you are to share. Many pastors think they're too busy to go to pastors conferences or mentor those just getting started. We're stewards of our influence as well as our physical possessions.

15. *Pour your life into a few people.* Invest in them to develop real leaders in the church and the kingdom at large.

16. *Cherish and protect friendships.*

17. *Give credit to other people.* Recognize your staff and coworkers. Give them praise and applause as worthy partners in ministry, always giving glory to God.

18. *Keep confidences.* Do not share with anyone what has been committed to you in privacy and confidentiality.

19. *Lead by example.* "Do as I say and not as I do" has never worked and never will.

20. *Practice servant leadership.* There are no prima donnas in God's service. We earn the right to lead as we serve God through those He places with us.

21. *When you're wrong, admit it.* "Forgive me" is a wonderful expression for pastors when necessary. I have had to apologize on more than one occasion for words and actions that were inappropriate in their spirit and content. Most people will readily accept such an acknowledgment when it is genuinely and freely given.

In February 2001, in recognition of 50 years in the ministry, his 65th birthday, and his 10th anniversary as president, Jimmy was honored by trustees with a surprise evening of celebration that included tributes from friends and family.

Terry Horton, a layman from First Baptist Church, Euless, and a longtime friend, said, "A man asked me the other day if I had a mentor. I said I did. He's my best friend. He's one of the busiest men I've ever been around in my life and yet he's always got time for people." Addressing Jimmy directly Horton said, "Your friendship makes me want to be a better Christian."

Elder son Randy Draper cited his father as a man of character, love, humor, and the ultimate servant. "Whether you know him from the outside or whether you know him from the inside like I do, he's the same."

In his report to the 2004 Southern Baptist Convention, Jimmy Draper shared two concerns he felt about the denomination's future: (1) four consecutive years of decline in baptisms and the reality that annual baptisms hadn't increased significantly since

1954; (2) the need to involve young ministers in leadership roles in associations, state conventions, and the SBC. "We can talk about all we've done to protect the integrity of Scripture, but if we don't pass along to the emerging generation the responsibility to carry it on, there will be no convention," Jimmy said. He repeated those concerns in a June 24 e-mail he titled, "Is the SBC a Frog in the Kettle?" Within twelve hours he had received more than one hundred e-mail responses, telling him, as he explained to Baptist Press, "that this has touched a nerve that resonates with folks across the country." In all, Jimmy heard from more than 350 ministers by letter and e-mail concerned about their lack of involvement in SBC life. They affirmed that his point was on target, offered suggestions, and thanked him for his leadership on the issue.

At the September 2004 meeting with LifeWay trustees, Jimmy emphasized the importance of embracing and implementing new ideas. He quoted British race car champion Stirling Moss: "To achieve anything you must be prepared to dabble on the boundary of disaster." Jimmy warned LifeWay trustees and employees, "We are nowhere as near that boundary as we need to be if we are going to design a LifeWay ten years in the future. We are way too conventional in our thinking, and we've got to break out of that."

He also cited the imperative of relying on God's guidance. "We've seen record growth over these past several years, but it scares me to wonder if I or anyone else at LifeWay has ever touched glory due God. So I ask myself, 'How will I respond to God when He one day asks me what kind of steward I was with the ministry He's given me here at LifeWay?' That's sobering. So much so it fuels a fire in me to completely give myself obediently to God's leading. I want you to know that I've got absolutely no intention to coast to the finish line of retirement."

By the fall of 2004 Jimmy had decided to officially announce his retirement at the February 2005 trustee meeting, effective no later than February 2006. He anticipated trustees creating a presidential search committee and selecting a successor by late summer or fall who could then work with him for a few months before he retired. At their fall retreat that year, Jimmy and Ted Warren made plans to equip the search committee for their task, analyzing and evaluating their administration, identifying strengths, tasks that were not completed, and suggested actions for consideration of a new administration. "I have no problems handing the reins to someone, and I want to do it graciously and enthusiastically. I want to help employees and everyone in the convention to be excited about the new president. I'm going to be his biggest cheerleader," Jimmy explained.

Looking ahead to what he would say in announcing his retirement, Jimmy emphasized, "I want to point to the optimism that exists for the future. I think we've got more things in place to accomplish some really significant milestones. I would not want there to be a glitch or disconnect. I want to focus on the fact that we're a strong organization, and we've learned how to grow business and revenues and, at the same time, manage expenses. We have really taken giant steps forward in technology.

"The new president will come into an organization that is expected not only to survive but to thrive," he continued. "People have been freed up to dream and to do some things that are exciting and do it in a way that is fiscally responsible as well as ministry-oriented. I think we have helped to deepen the understanding of the ministry-business tension that we have. It's a good tension, and we don't ever want to get away from that."

While the new president and leadership team would, of course, establish their own goals, Jimmy hoped they would carry on with some tasks he would not have time to see to completion: helping ethnic churches more, becoming more competitive in music products, further improving technology, building international markets and outreach, and the list goes on.

However it changes in the years ahead, Jimmy is confident LifeWay will remain the servant of the convention it has always been. He notes, "We are the rope that holds Southern Baptists together, whether they realize it or not. That's a thread that has run from the very beginning, due to the wisdom of the people that began the work, that we help to communicate who the denomination is and what we believe. I think that tie to the churches is something that needs to continue into the future because nobody else has it."

Looking back over his years of service, Jimmy hopes he and his colaborers will be remembered for "helping create a culture where people were freed up to work, that we helped people exercise their gifts to the best of their ability and to follow the will of the Lord in their calling, that we cared about churches and people, and did our best to help pastors. I would like us to be seen as a servant organization that is a business but utilizes its funds to help minister to churches and church leaders. I also wish our denominational emphasis on authority of Scripture had translated into more aggressive evangelism here in America. I think we're better, but we're not as good as we could be. We have a long way to go, and evangelism is one of those areas. Our denomination's greatest future threat is conflict within churches that causes them to turn inward and away from the challenge of carrying out the Great Commission in their communities and around the world."

When asked about plans for his retirement years, Jimmy smiled and said he was more focused on finishing well at LifeWay. Retirement for Jimmy Draper will alter his emphasis but not his pace. There will still be children to enjoy and grandchildren to spoil; still a host of friends and colleagues in ministry to visit, share ideas with, inspire and be inspired by. He and Carol Ann will still enjoy their customary visits to Hawaii twice a year on Jimmy's frequent-flyer miles, where Jimmy will continue playing the fastest round of golf any of his partners have ever seen.

Expect to see the two of them back at First Baptist Church in Euless, where many hundreds of friends still worship, and where the families of all three children will be nearby. Expect to see Brother Jimmy back in the pulpit and on the mission field preaching the gospel and winning souls for Christ.

And expect to see a smile on his face as one of the most honored denominational leaders of his generation feels the same exultation in the pulpit–and the same passion for Jesus and the world–as he felt that Labor Day weekend in 1950 when the Lord preached through him for the very first time. A half century and more have made the experience all the richer, and the promise of the future all the brighter.

ACKNOWLEDGMENTS

T WO TREASURIES OF INFORMATION made this book possible. The first was Jimmy Draper's remarkably complete and organized personal files going back almost forty-five years. I had unlimited access to everything both public and private, and owe a debt of thanks to Jimmy for his kindness and to Carol Ann for her hospitality during the days I camped out upstairs or in the garage and made my way through box after box.

The second was the family members, friends, and colleagues who gave so generously of their time to talk about Jimmy to me, adding the personal insights and details that make a book like this come to life. Again I thank Jimmy and Carol Ann, neither of whom ever turned down an interview request nor wearied of explaining some long-ago adventure time after time until I got it straight.

Thanks also to those members of the family who shared their stories: sons Bailey and Randy, and daughter Terri Draper Wilkinson; brother Charlie and sister-in-law Retta, who drove down from Louisville for a personal interview and a taste of Loveless fried chicken; and brother George's widow, Beverly, who kindly carved the time out of her hectic schedule.

Special thanks as well to Dr. Gene Mims of the LifeWay board of trustees, who has been a great encourager to me in the past, and to Dr. Paige Patterson, president of Southwestern Baptist Theological Seminary.

Others who supplied essential pieces for this mosaic include Mary Betts, Howard Cargill, Bob Eklund, Frank and Shirley Favazza, Freddie Gage, George Harris, Terry Horton, Charles Martin, Marilyn Novak, Todd Smith, and Charles Thornton. They have been faithful keepers of the flame of living history.

On the practical side of things I'm grateful for the friendship and support of the people at Broadman & Holman who helped bring this project to life: publisher David Shepherd, editorial director Len Goss, project editor John Landers, and to Lisa Parnell for producing the photo section. They have cheered me on throughout the process and been an unfailing source of wisdom and common sense. No writer could ask for more.

SOURCES

M OST OF THE INFORMATION and quotations in this book are from interviews with Dr. Draper, his family and friends, and from his exhaustive file of notes, clippings, and correspondence dating back to the 1950s. Following are the most important supplemental sources used. Particularly helpful were the books by Pressler and Sutton; Hefley's series is also noteworthy.

Arrington, Mike, personal interview.

"Baptist factions try, fail to halt power struggle." *Fort Worth Star-Telegram*, October 3, 1984.

"Baptist Faith and Message: A Statement Adopted by the Southern Baptist Convention, June 14, 2000." Nashville: LifeWay Christian Resources, 2000.

Barnes, William Wright. *The Southern Baptist Convention 1845–1953*. Nashville: Broadman Press, 1954.

"Baylor changes charter; 'regents' will govern." *The Baptist Standard*, September 26, 1990.

"Baylor Charter Change Thwarts Threatened Takeover by Presslerite-Fundamentalists." *Baylor Needs* You! newsletter, n.d.

"Baylor's McCall," *Scene Magazine,* in *The Dallas Morning News*, February 22, 1981.

"Broadman & Holman Publishers announce new Bible translation." Baptist Press, May 7, 1999.

Brown, John. *The Pilgrim Fathers of New England and their Puritan Successors,* Pasadena, Texas: Pilgrim Publications, 1970.

"Celebrating the Life and Ministry of Jimmy Draper" event program, February 12, 2001.

"Charter and Bylaws of Baylor University" pamphlet.

Criswell, W. A. *Why I Preach that the Bible Is Literally True.* Nashville: Broadman & Holman Publishers, 1995 [originally published 1969].

Davies, G. Henton. *Genesis.* Broadman Bible Commentary, Nashville: Broadman Press, 1969.

Draper, Benjamin Poff. *Some Genealogical Notes for the Descendants of Benjamin Franklin Draper 1846–1929 Together with a Record of His Ancestors in the United States from 1647 and His Descendants to 1960.* San Francisco, privately published, 1959.

"Draper: Baptisms, young ministers' involvement are cause for concern." Baptist Press, June 16, 2004.

"Draper calls SSB past a prelude to future." Baptist Press, August 21, 1991.

Draper, Cecil Mead. "A Branch of the Draper Family, with Short Sketches of Allied Families: Peden, Allen, Thrailkill. " Denver: privately published, 1969.

"Draper challenges leaders, trustees to intensify LifeWay's support of evangelism effort." Baptist Press, September 16, 2004.

"Draper, Hultgren receive L. R. Scarborough awards." Baptist Press, October 25, 1999.

Draper, James T., Jr. *Authority: The Critical Issue for Southern Baptists.* Old Tappan, NJ: Fleming H. Revell Company, 1984.

Draper, James T., Jr., and Kenneth Keathley. *Biblical Authority: The Critical Issue for the Body of Christ.* Nashville: Broadman & Holman Publishers, 2001.

Draper, Jimmy. *Faith That Works: Studies in James.* Keller, Texas: HeartSpring Media, 1999.

Draper, Jimmy [James T., Sr.]. "Memoranda Book." Unpublished diary, 1926.

"Draper: Now is the time to show 'a new day is dawning.'" Baptist Press, June 28, 2004.

"Draper presented E. Y. Mullins award at Southern Seminary." Baptist Press, October 21, 1998.

Elliott, Ralph H. *The Message of Genesis.* Nashville: Broadman Press, 1961.

"Euless Church may seek rain through prayer." *Fort Worth Star-Telegram,* July 8, 1980.

"Expresses 'Our Deep Commitment.'" *Ohio Baptist Messenger,* June 6, 1985.

"Feuding by Southern Baptists intensifies." *The Houston Post,* June 1, 1985.

"FAITH: Former Green Beret launches soul-saving offensive." Baptist Press, January 28, 1998.

"Finance and Business Services Division, Most Important Events, 1994–2003." PowerPoint slides prepared for LifeWay trustee meeting, February 9, 2004.

"FIRST PERSON: Is the SBC a frog in the kettle?" Baptist Press, June 24, 2004.

"Friends mark Jimmy Draper milestones: 10 years at LifeWay, 50 in ministry." Baptist Press, February 13, 2001.

"Holman Christian Standard Bible dedicated; described as historic, accurate, readable." Baptist Press, April 5, 2004.

"James T. Draper Chair of Pastoral Ministries at Southwestern Baptist Theological Seminary," brochure.

Hefley, James C. *The Truth in Crisis, Vol. 1: The Controversy in the Southern Baptist Convention*. Dallas: Criterion Publications, 1986.

———. *The Truth in Crisis, Vol. 2: Bringing the Controversy Up-to-Date*. Dallas: Criterion Publications, 1987.

———. *The Truth in Crisis, Vol. 3: Conservative Resurgence or Political Takeover?* Hannibal, Mo.: Hannibal Books, 1988.

———. *The Truth in Crisis, Vol. 4: The 'State' of the Denomination*. Hannibal, Mo.: Hannibal Books, 1989.

Humphreys, Kirk, telephone interview.

"Judge Abner McCall." *Baylor: The Magazine of Baylor University*, April/May, 1985.

"Leaders say Dilday faces firing attempt," *Fort Worth Star-Telegram*, March 22, 1985.

"Leaving pastorate represents identity change for Draper." Baptist Press, August 9, 1991.

"LifeWay trustees approve new division, elect vice president for technology." Baptist Press, February 13, 2002.

"Lose Self in Mission SBC Leader's Plea." *Southwestern News*, October, 1982.

"The Magic Word: Inerrancy." *The Baptist Messenger*, May 31, 1979.

McBeth, Leon, *Celebrating Heritage and Hope*, unpublished centennial history of the Baptist Sunday School Board, 1990.

Pressler, Paul. *A Hill on Which to Die: One Southern Baptist's Journey*. Nashville: Broadman & Holman Publishers, 1999.

Reccord, Robert, e-mailed statement.

Reedy, Virginia L. *People in His Purpose: An Eighty-five Year History of First Baptist Church, Euless, Texas 1904–1989*. Euless: First Baptist Church, Euless, 1988.

"Reynolds' Ramblings." *Baylor University Items*, January 28, 1980.

Scott, Mark, personal interview.

Sherman, Cecil. "The 'New Baptists.'" *The Baylor Line*, September, 1985.

Sons of the American Revolution Application for Membership, March 15, 1979.

"SSB trustee meeting called regarding Elder's presidency." Baptist Press, January 14, 1991.

Sullivan, James L. "My Administration Philosophy." September 11, 1991.

Sullivan, John, e-mailed statement.

Sutton, Jerry. *The Baptist Reformation: The Conservative Resurgence in the Southern Baptist Convention*. Nashville: Broadman & Holman Publishers, 2001.

"SWBTS trustees table move to silence Dilday." *Baptist and Reflector*, October 24, 1984.

"The War for Thee University." *Texas Monthly*, November, 1991.

"Tim Vineyard named director of LifeWay E-Business Group." Baptist Press, March 20, 2000.

"Trustees adopt record 2005116 operating budget, approve fast-track business plan for conference centers." Baptist Press, September 16, 2004.

"Warren praises employees for 'remarkable' turnaround." *Boardcast: A Newsletter for Sunday School Board Employees*, October 4, 1995.

Warren, Ted, personal interview.